THE PRIVATE LIFE
OF
PUBLIC FINANCE

PLATFORM

PRESS

Bucks County
Pennsylvania

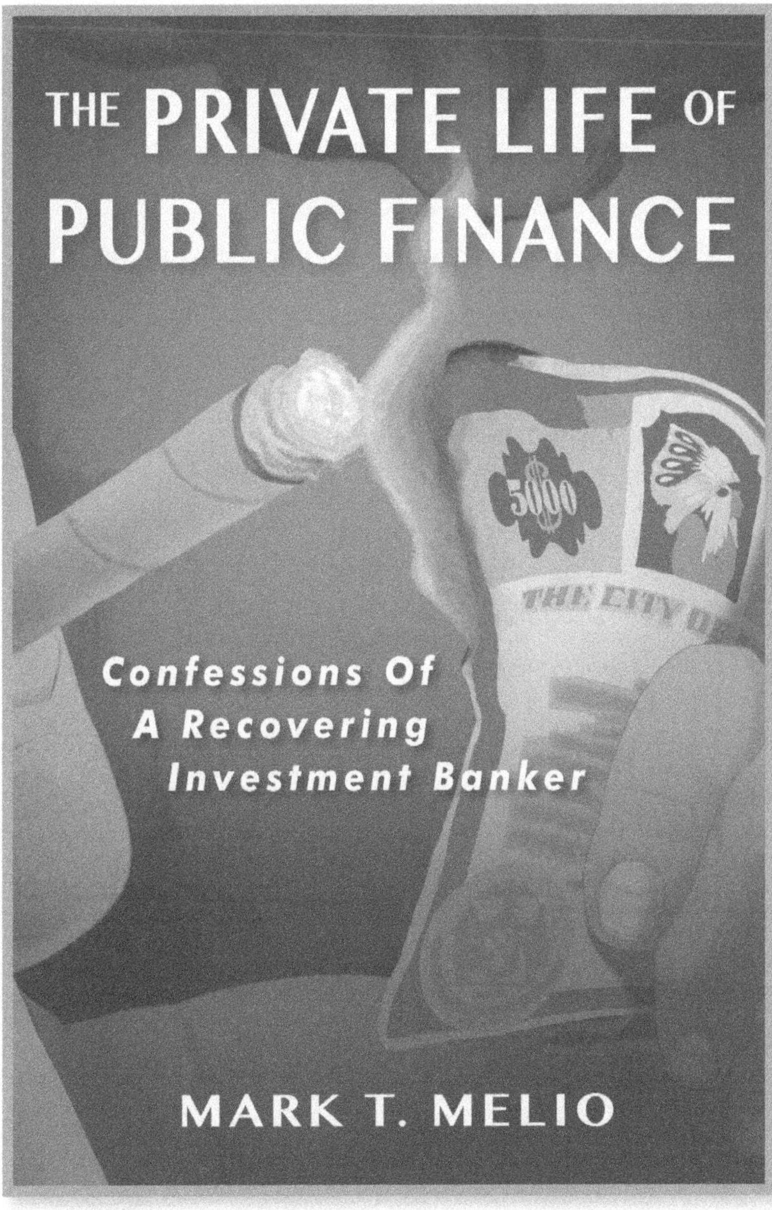
THE PRIVATE LIFE OF
PUBLIC FINANCE
Confessions Of
A Recovering
Investment Banker
MARK T. MELIO

Copies are available at special discounts for bulk purchases in the
United States by corporations, institutions, and other organizations.
For more information, please contact the publisher.

Cover art by Louisiana Ramos
Line drawings by Drew DeBakker
Author photo by Linda Bergonia

Editorial, production, and publishing services provided by
Platform Press
Winans Kuenstler Publishing, LLC
93 East Court Street
Doylestown, Pennsylvania 18901
(215) 500-1989
www.WKPublishing.com

Printed in the United States

ISBN: 978-0-9974930-1-6

1 2 3 4 5 6 7 8 9 0
First Trade Paperback Edition

In memory of J. Patrick Sheehan,
who always had his priorities in order
and never missed a beat.

TABLE OF CONTENTS

*"What's breaking into a bank
compared to founding one?"*

From *The Threepenny Opera* by Bertolt Brecht

INTRODUCTION

I am a recovering investment banker, but you shouldn't feel sorry for me. I was happy as an investment banker, successful by any measure. I'm just a lot happier and more fulfilled now that I'm sitting on the other side of the table.

This is a book I could not have written while I worked for any securities firm and kept my job. Today I work for the investment banks' customers instead of the bank. Now I'm on the outside looking in, except I have a good idea what's going on inside the bank.

That means I can finally tell the story of what it was really like to be near the epicenter of the financial universe during the best and worst of recent times. I can add my perspective to that of many others about how that many-headed beast we call Wall Street became the second-most distrusted of all industry groups, just barely edging out the media. Apparently, the only thing people find worse than lying is stealing. Or maybe it's lying about stealing.

Either way, the bottom of that public perception barrel was

my world for nearly a quarter-century and the reputation was hard-earned. Beginning in the mid-1980s (think *Wall Street*, *Die Hard*, *Working Girl*, *Goodfellas*, *Bonfire Of The Vanities*, and *Do The Right Thing*), I was an investment banker at two of the financial industry's most fabled and most vilified institutions. For ten years I worked at Goldman Sachs & Co., founded almost 150 years ago, followed by twelve years at J.P. Morgan & Co. (now JPMorgan Chase), founded more than 200 years ago.

Although I was in the investment banking deal business all that time, it was in a relatively sleepy corner of Wall Street that rarely makes headlines but affects every single American's daily life. My specialty—public finance—involves the sale of large municipal bond offerings by investment banks on behalf of public and not-for-profit institutional clients.

Your new county courthouse, the reconstruction of the city bridge that was about to fall down, the modernization of your local airport, or the expansion of your college alma mater's football stadium—these were all likely financed by the issuance and sale of municipal bonds. Those bonds are bought by investors looking for income that is low-risk (governments and taxpayer-financed agencies rarely go out of business) and tax-exempt—investors don't have to pay taxes on the interest income. Within public finance, the focus of my career has been healthcare.

Every time you pay a toll, your water bill, local taxes, or get a knee replacement at your community hospital, you're investing in that part of Wall Street—public finance. The dominant issues in my field include mergers of hospitals into regional and national systems, the employment of physicians, managing the risks and costs of maintaining a health plan, and all the other developments in how we finance our healthcare infrastructure. It may not sound sexy, but those of us on the inside get a glimpse into the future of everyone's healthcare, and we're often among the first to hear about the latest medical discoveries and treatments. That makes what we do more exciting than it may seem at first glance.

Because my work on Wall Street was outside the spotlight of mega corporate deals and the rapacious or manipulative trading schemes that got the world into so much trouble, I enjoyed the unique position and perspective of being in that world but not entirely of it. What I saw during those years was a slow but steady slide from a business where the top values were personal reputation, integrity, and putting clients' interests first to what it is today—a coldly efficient money machine that's shifted virtually all the risk from itself to its customers.

Before the 1980s, the most important litmus test of a transaction or deal was first whether it was ethical and, if so, was it legal. By the late 1990s, if the lawyers said Wall Street could do it and get away with it—deeming a particular tactic technically legal—then it became automatically ethical. That sort of economic Darwinism or legal cat-and-mouse helped produce the Great Meltdown of 2008, this generation's version of the Great Crash of 1929. The wreckage it left behind, wreckage that we're still living with eight years later, taught us that just because it was legal to bundle shaky mortgages into saleable, overpriced securities didn't mean it was a good idea.

Like its famous predecessor, the Great Recession will be remembered as one of Wall Street's great betrayals. Like last time, it happened by gambling the country's wealth and losing, thus putting a torpedo into so many American Dreams.

Thirty years ago the leading firms were privately owned and run by groups of partners who had their own money on the table, right beside their customers'. The firms that survived the slaughter of 2008 are today publicly held, heavily regulated, badgered by shareholders, stalked by rivals, ruled by ambitious managers who are henpecked by compliance, legal, and human resource executives, and defined by computer algorithms. No matter what the slogan says, maximizing the bank's profit and minimizing its risk comes first, not customers.

That, in a nutshell, is the breaking bad story of Wall Street and how the big investment banks were able to drive the world economy into a ditch. Unlike the partners of the past whose wealth and good names stood shoulder to shoulder with their customers', modern CEOs seem to come and go with the seasons. Whether they walk away as heroes, or crawl away as failures, the departure is nearly always with pockets full of gold and a soft landing at another bank. Wall Street's captains never seem to go down with the ship. Their yachts are there to pluck them from the waves and ferry them off to their next commands.

The raw material and the end product of the investment business is the same—money. Money goes in one end and a little bit less money comes out the other. The firms who raise and handle money take a slice each time it changes hands. That's how Wall Street firms make their livings, whether it's corporate or public finance. The faster money moves, the more slices the banks get to keep. If it sounds a little like a scam, you aren't alone. As playwright Bertolt Brecht wrote in 1928 (*The Threepenny Opera*), the easiest way to rob a bank is to start one.

Not all investment bankers are alike. There is a caste system within the firms. The difference between putting together an international pharmaceutical mega-merger versus structuring municipal bonds to build a new hospital inpatient tower is the difference between a one-night stand and getting married. Whether or not a Facebook or an Amazon ever earns a penny, whether or not investors lose their shirts on an Enron or a WorldCom, the investment bankers who provided fairness opinions, and their trading desks who managed the sale of shares, made their money up front. Like sharks, once their bellies were full they immediately swam off in search of the next meal.

Raising the funds to build a children's hospital, on the other hand, feels like a calling to those of us who earn our living doing it. A high percentage of the public finance bankers I have known and worked with actually have hearts and consciences. Whereas the relationship between banker and client in corporate finance is driven mostly by deals, our public finance clients often became long-term friends. We share with them a sense of purpose and pride in helping fund better healthcare.

A few hospital and university executives who've sat on the other side of the desk from me wore a priest's collar or a nun's habit. Great care goes into transactions when, like me, you were raised to be a good Catholic boy and your client is the Sisters of Mercy, or Georgetown University, or the University of Notre Dame. They don't carry rulers like my teachers did, but they don't have to.

It's now 2016 and the dust is finally settling from the Great Recession. The banks that were too big to fail are once again obscenely profitable. College grads who were too young to understand why Mom and Dad had to sell the house for less than it was worth are showing renewed interest in working on Wall Street.

Since the financial crisis, the percentage of students choosing to go into finance has fallen at premier schools like Carnegie Mellon, MIT, and Harvard—they're going to Silicon Valley. Nevertheless, Wall Street remains the top destination at many business schools. In the summer of 2014, for instance, Morgan Stanley said it received 90,000 applications for 1,000 entry-level jobs. The allure of potential wealth—a life of luxury and privilege—remains irresistible.

Unlike previous generations attracted to the bright lights and the big city, today's young people express a strong desire to make the world a better place. It's a noble idea but a paradox on Wall Street where it's all about the money. It's a brutally competitive business and only the most competitive types of people on the planet succeed.

Those of us who fish in Wall Street's calmer waters—selling municipal bonds for state and local governments that provide public services and for not-for-profits that run hospitals and universities—are also competitive. In the pecking order within the firms, however, the public finance bankers are the high school freshmen and the corporate bankers are the seniors who delight in mocking and pranking them.

One year at Goldman Sachs, the fixed income and staid municipal bond departments were going through a rough patch while the folks in the tailored suits and red suspenders—the gunslingers in equities and in mergers and acquisitions—were riding a boom. During a break in a compliance meeting around that time, my public finance colleagues and I found the men's room urinals decorated with hand-lettered signs. A sign reading "Equities" had been taped on the wall over each urinal except the shorty for boys, which read "Fixed Income and Munis." It was funny and insulting at the same time, like a good prank should be.

The common attraction for anyone in the investment banking business is the prospect of making a handsome income and enjoying the trappings of privilege. The universal requirement is to make as much money as possible for the bank (and therefore, yourself), no matter how big your heart or how resolute your conscience.

The sort of people who go into my field understand that they are unlikely to make a killing. Public finance bankers tend to be less interested in getting rich and are more motivated by pride. They'd like to do well, but not at the expense of doing good.

Like many of my peers, I have often enjoyed a sense of accomplishment when I've had the occasion to drive past a state-of-the-art neurological center or a new hospital wing and say to my kids, "Look! Over there! Your Dad helped build that."

My decision to tell the story of Wall Street as I experienced it was inspired by having seen the financial industry from both sides, first as a banker and now as an advocate and fiduciary for my clients. I'm in the unique position of knowing which cards everyone is holding.

As an independent financial advisor, my firm and I represent many premier healthcare institutions across the country. I get to work with some of the same people I knew when I represented the banks and they were my customers. Then my obligation to the bank was to drum up as much profitable business as possible. My clients trusted me and the banks I worked for to deal with them honestly and fairly. Unfortunately, and with personal chagrin, I have to admit that certain industry practices that I'll describe later did not, and still don't, deserve that trust. At least now I can try to do something about it.

Since leaving Wall Street in 2009 (it felt more like being pushed off a cliff), I've been using what I know to help steer my clients around the pitfalls and get them the capital they need on the best terms at the lowest cost. It is, in many ways, the best of both worlds for someone with my background.

Public finance may lack the sex appeal of the latest social networking fad, but if you're curious to hear an insider's account of why and how our financial system broke down, and how it's still broken in some respects, I hope you'll keep reading.

If you are a young person contemplating a career in investment banking, I hope you'll understand why I strongly suggest you explore other careers before taking such a leap. Wall Street is not the real world. People in it often feel entitled to behave in ways that most of us would regard as shameful, wasteful, and callous. You quickly get seduced by the money and prestige and get caught up in the relentless competitive pursuit of more of both. Once you're in, it's very hard to give it up. For some people it becomes a destructive addiction.

For those responsible for managing the institutions that make up our healthcare infrastructure, I hope to continue to contribute to the discussion and debate about the rapid changes taking place in how healthcare is managed and financed. The biggest systems are getting bigger and more complex every day. So are their challenges. The trend seems destined to continue for some time.

Finally, for those now working on Wall Street or soon to be, I hope some of what you read here will get you thinking about how you define success. I made my pact with the devil for almost twenty-five years and for much of that time I enjoyed the perks and pride of representing firms with long, storied histories. I was happy and successful. I liked my clients and I worked hard for them as well as for the bank.

But I'm a lot happier now on the other side of the table.

—Mark T. Melio
Winnetka, Illinois, 2016

CHAPTER 1:
KILL 'EM WITH KINDNESS

Kissing Tony taught me the most important skill required to become a successful investment banker. Tony was a steelworker with a high school diploma who had a lot of heart and charisma. Without intending to at first, he evolved into a community leader in the 1960s.

He was first an elected commissioner on the board that governed a good part of Levittown, Pennsylvania, the post-World War II suburb that for generations defined the middle class. A lifelong Democrat in a Democratic district, he only lost one election, in 1972, the year of the Nixon landslide. Four years later, Tony ran again and the voters took him right back.

After two decades of local politics, he was elected to the House of Representatives for the Commonwealth of Pennsylvania, a full-time legislature. He retired from U.S. Steel's Fairless Works and subsequently won twelve elections in a row. By the time Kissing Tony retired from politics in 2010, he'd logged nearly a half century as an elected official, known to generations of aspirational working-class constituents as one of their own. No problem was too small for his attention and his problem-solving skills.

They called him Kissing Tony because he kissed almost everybody—men, women, and children—and hugged the rest. He was warm-hearted and irresistible and made others feel cared about. He became so well known for his affectionate greetings that near the end of his career, his staff had buttons made up that they'd pin on the lapels of people he'd smooched: "I was kissed by Tony Melio." When he died a few years ago, one of his statehouse colleagues joked, "Nobody in heaven is safe from Tony's kisses."

He was first generation Italian-American, raised in an Italian-speaking home in a proud working-class neighborhood in Trenton, New Jersey, a factory town. The kissing went along with the expressive hand gestures and animated facial expressions that are unmistakably Italian, social customs his parents brought with them from the old country.

Everybody loved Kissing Tony and Kissing Tony loved his constituents. I loved him more than anyone. He was my father and by example he taught me to take an interest in everyone you meet. He taught my brother, Jay, my sister, Sheri, and me to be good listeners, keep our cool in a crisis, be active problem solvers, get along with as many folks as possible, say our prayers, and, hardest of all, shrug off the inevitable sticks and stones that opponents might throw at us.

"You can't let your opponents see that they've gotten to you or else they've won," he said. "Stay calm, cool, and collected. Kill 'em with kindness. It will drive them nuts."

Another invaluable bit of advice that stayed with me was, "Listen to everyone. There is always a lesson to be learned from people's stories." And, "There are three sides to every story."

What I learned in college and in my first jobs in economics and accounting helped prepare me for the theory and mechanics of investment banking. My father, Anthony Melio, showed me how to do it well. My mother, Anna May, showed me how to do it with integrity.

My parents and grandparents were very much on my mind on the day in April 1987 when I began my career on Wall Street. After hours of intensive orientation meetings, I found myself with a few quiet moments alone to process this dramatic turning point in my life. Standing before a wall of huge plate-glass windows on a high floor in the corporate offices of Goldman Sachs—just a few blocks from the New York Stock Exchange—my gaze swept the jumble of Lower Manhattan's peaks and canyons.

Beyond all those buildings, the horizon was filled with the panorama of New York Harbor with the Verrazano Bridge just visible through the haze. It was like an opening film scene, calling for a sound track of Frank Sinatra crooning "New York, New York." The World Trade Center towers punctuated the downtown skyline like a couple of giant exclamation points. Beyond it the Statue of Liberty stood on her pedestal at the headwaters of the bay, backlit by the setting sun, holding her torch out toward the sea.

I'm sure thousands have had the same thought I did on their first day at a fabled institution like Goldman Sachs. This really IS the center of the known financial universe! Wall Street! How the hell did I manage to get here?

In the harbor, closer to Manhattan than the Statue, I could make out the dark outlines of Ellis Island. The lights of Brooklyn and Hoboken revealed the towers on the abandoned immigration complex. It had been closed for a quarter century by then and the jumble of shadowy structures resembled the decaying factories that I'd seen from the commuter train between Trenton and New York.

A wave of emotion swept over me as I imagined my grandparents and great-grandparents—clutching cloth overcoats against the cold sea air—emerging from the iron belly of a smoky steamship as it glided the final mile or so to its berth. It would have been the welcome end of an exhausting ten-day voyage that started in Naples with separation and tears and ended with an uncertain but hopeful future.

With the other storm-tossed souls and huddled masses, they would have wept, laughed, hugged, and pointed at the enormous gentle face gazing out to sea like the mother of all saints. What a long and improbable family narrative, I thought. Here I was, crisply turned out in my new best suit and tie, peering down from the ramparts of wealth and privilege, just a mile and a half from the site of that modest but defining moment in my family's history.

Out of the gate, I knew I would never become a "master of the universe" like the cutthroat bond traders portrayed by author Tom Wolfe in his novel *The Bonfire Of The Vanities*—profanely wheeling and dealing and cutting corners on the way to great wealth or ruin. It wasn't in my blood or experience. Nor was it my ambition. If I was a wonky nerd, at least I was a wonky nerd at Goldman Sachs, an old, well-established firm with a colorful history and international reputation.

Whatever the future held, I would always remember that as the moment I first stepped through the looking glass into the parallel universe of Wall Street, where many things are bigger or smaller than they appear.

As I gazed out that window I paid silent tribute to all my forbearers—my father's from Italy and my mother's from Czechoslovakia—who had made so many sacrifices for the generations that followed. I vowed I would never take it for granted and always make them proud.

My Italian grandmother's journey began in a hamlet near the Gran Sasso mountains in the Abruzzo region. Addolorata (Dorothy) was twelve when she came to the States. When I was growing up, she worked at a Bayer Aspirin factory filling bottles with pills. I spent many weekends with my beloved Nana in her kitchen, learning family traditions and how to cook.

My Italian grandfather's family came from Naples. Giuseppe's (Joseph's) mother had fiery red hair, told fortunes, and had been married several times. The family settled in central New Jersey near Trenton, where my grandfather was a track-layer and laborer for the Pennsylvania Railroad.

My mother's father, Mike, worked in a factory making industrial rubber products. He had been working since he was a kid, after his mother died. My mother's mother, Anna, cleaned offices at night in the state capitol building downtown and had the most generous heart of anyone I've ever known.

My father drove trucks and operated cranes at U.S. Steel's Fairless Works in Bucks County, Pennsylvania for thirty years. My mother was a secretary in the New Jersey state government, and later an office manager for the Touche Ross office in Trenton.

My family on both sides had worked hard at hard jobs to make a better life for us all. But when I'd talk about going to college, my grandparents, especially my grandmothers, would shake their heads woefully and wag a finger.

"You learn a trade, like your uncle and your cousins. This education thing, God knows what you can do with that. Madonna mia! People always need a plumber. They always need an electrician. They always need carpenters."

It was funny, but I played along. "But with a college education," I said, "I can make just as good a living using my head."

"You should still learn a trade. It's to fall back on, just in case."

My great-uncle was a carpentry contractor. When family members needed something fixed or built, they called on him. When he was around, my grandmothers would tell me to go watch him work and "learn a thing or two you could actually use." I did learn a thing or two, just not what they had in mind.

One day when I was about six, my mother took me with her shopping. She was paying for her purchases at the checkout when I noticed a display rack full of magazines. I bent over, put my hands on my knees like my great-uncle, and yelped, "Jeeeeeeeee-sus Christ! Look at all these books!"

Thus ended my carpentry apprenticeship.

My father, on the other hand, was someone I loved to watch, working in his position as a public official. He stumbled into the role because our house sat right on the dividing line between two townships. Neither was plowing our street in the winter or fixing our potholes in the summer. In the process of going to town halls and badgering people to get these things done, he became the de facto neighborhood spokesman, and that led to elected office.

When I was about eight years old he began taking me with him to township meetings where I'd quietly sit and watch him interact with other officials, the public, and the reporters. He often spoke to me before the meetings about how certain people think, what was important to them, and how he would try to make compromises and work through disputes. And on the way home he'd explain what happened. I loved being his little body man and confidant.

Because of his position and his accessibility, people were always calling him at home about one problem or another. The callers were often anxious, irate, or just loony. But in those days before caller ID and answering machines, he couldn't just ignore a ringing phone. It might be a real emergency. So at a tender age, I became my father's call screener.

When the phone rang, my father in the living room reading the paper and my mother in the kitchen would simultaneously yell, "Mark!" Unless I had instructions otherwise, I always began with, "I'm sorry. My dad's not home." Then I'd listen to the caller tell me their story of woe or frustration. Many were people who had too much time on their hands: "What's he going to do about that buzzing noise from the high-tension wires? Can't they turn that off?"

It wasn't that he didn't want to talk with them. We just knew that if he got on the phone he'd be too polite to hang up and then be on it all night. If he could tell from my end of the conversation that it was someone he wanted to talk to, he would give me a signal to take a message and then he'd call them back. After each call I'd recount what was said. He wanted to know all the details. That helped sharpen my listening and memory skills and enhanced my storytelling.

It was a circus and an education. I learned one of many valuable lessons about people. Just listening to them complain would often end with them solving their own problem or deciding to live with it. The more my father just listened to people, the more people liked him. It worked for me as well. People would hang up after telling me how smart and wise I was for such a little boy when I hadn't said ten words.

I remembered all of that years later when I was at Goldman Sachs and we had a partner in charge of the municipal bond department who was a relentless talker. In conversations with him, the less you said the more he thought you agreed with him.

In recruiting season, if my colleagues and I liked a particular candidate we would make sure he or she got in to see that partner. During the interview we'd walk by his glass-walled office to see how it was going. Inevitably he'd be talking and gesticulating and the poor recruit would just be sitting there trying to look interested. Afterward the partner would come out of his office gushing to us, "That's one smart guy! Terrific! We should hire him."

The influences that shaped my self-image include my parents' example, my Catholic upbringing and education, and my feeling of responsibility as the third parent—my younger brother and sister were born when I was nine and ten years old. My parents were a perfect fit for my personality and I was determined to be their ideal kid. I became an Eagle Scout, was elected president of my class, and over-achieved in my studies.

My mother gets the credit for instilling the most important value—integrity. She was the moral compass, keeping a watchful eye on my father to make sure he stuck to the straight and narrow. She'd seen many of the men in her family go astray in one way or another and wasn't about to let that happen to him.

When I was about nine, she sat me down at the kitchen table and told me a story about my dad that became legendary in my family's narrative. It bloomed in my youthful mind into a parable about life.

From an early age my father always had some sort of job. Before he was hired by U.S. Steel for its brand-new plant on the Delaware River, he worked in a grocery store in Trenton's predominantly Italian Chambersburg neighborhood. He loved cars and saved up the money to buy a flashy new Chrysler DeSoto, circa 1955, with sweeping tail fins and tons of chrome. He was getting out of it one day when two suits walked briskly up to the door.

"Where'd you get this car?" one snarled.

The other suit chuckled. "Yeah, where'd a grocery clerk get the dough for a set of wheels like that?"

They told my dad that he needed to come to the office of the FBI, on the fourth floor of the post office in downtown Trenton—the Federal building.

"We want to talk to you. This Saturday, two o'clock. We'll be waiting and you better show up if you know what's good for you. You better have a good story to tell about that car, too."

My father had nothing to hide. He had his bank book to show he saved the money and a receipt for the car. He shrugged it off. Besides, he didn't recall the post office having four floors. He thought it might have been a prank but he showed up on time anyway to discover there WAS a fourth floor and that the agents were waiting to pounce.

They told him they were investigating an uncle of his who was "into some bad stuff, and we think you might be in on it, too." They showed him a book full of photos of men, some of whom he knew but most of whom he didn't, and tried to double-talk him into saying something incriminating or useful. But my father was clueless and the agents soon realized it and sent him home. The FBI eventually found enough evidence of some lawbreaking because his uncle ended up in prison.

After my mother told me the story, my father told his version, adding in details and confessing, "Marco, I was scared shitless. I did nothing wrong, but they tried to make me feel like I had."

Years later, when he ran for office and became a township commissioner, he often found himself dealing with shady characters looking for favorable zoning decisions, jobs, or contracts. Some offered money, some offered favors.

My father's door—our door—was always open, so my mother had a chance to overhear some of these conversations. My father dutifully reported the rest. When she heard something that sounded fishy or illegal, she'd tell him, "You stay away from him. He's no good."

As his Jiminy Cricket, my mother had keen political instincts. My father's constituency was reliably Democratic but the local newspaper was owned by Republicans. The paper was always looking for any scrap of controversy that might stain his career and make him vulnerable. Even if my father had ever been tempted to cross the line, my mother's emotional, high-volume rants on the subject would have been a guaranteed deterrent.

Sometimes she gave him no choice. At dinner he might casually mention, "They're having a municipal officials conference in Miami this winter. It's sponsored by one of the trash haulers. It won't cost a cent and you can go with me."

"What? Are you kidding? No how!" she'd yell. "We're not going. You're not going. Who gives a free vacation for nothing? Nobody you want to know, that's who!"

When he became a state representative, the inducements were more elaborate—"business development" junkets to Europe. On the rare occasion that she relented—the conference had to be in Pennsylvania—she made him swear he would attend every single session and she'd quiz him about it all when he got back. My dad could be a stubborn, strong-willed guy, but he was no match for my mother's vigilance and passion.

The thing that got her the most aggravated was any attack on my father's integrity. Growing up in politics, the worst times were always the elections. No matter how good a public servant my father was, no matter how many people he helped, someone would always come out of the woodwork to falsely accuse him of some wrongdoing or twist a vote into something it wasn't.

If he voted for a tax increase he was fiscally irresponsible, soaking the public. If he voted for budget cuts, they said he was hurting programs that feed homeless children, or something like that.

My father was reluctant to speak out when someone was throwing political mud. Initially, he may have been embarrassed about his lack of a college education and self-conscious about his command of language. His shyness turned out to be an advantage and he had learned how to make it part of a calculated strategy to win people over and defuse disputes. He avoided getting into public shoving matches. This drove my mother nuts.

"You've got to get out there and fight back. You can't just let people run around telling lies!"

"What can I say? Either way, it'll get twisted to sound like what they want."

In the end, my father's instincts served him well. Being quiet and letting his opponents have a one-sided argument made them look like blowhards, liars, or crazy. He defanged his enemies with silence, tolerance, and even kindness.

By the time I arrived on Wall Street, I'd had about twenty years' experience watching the sport of politics. While other boys were riding their bikes or playing street hockey, I was listening to lawyers presenting arguments in a zoning hearing. My extended family included the township manager and the police chief. Grown-ups treated me like a short adult and I regarded them as tall children. I loved every minute of it.

Like the other members of my immediate family, I always had some sort of job. The summer between my first and second year of college I worked six days a week in a dusty, dirty, noisy wallboard factory in Trenton. A number of my coworkers had been on that assembly line for twenty or more years—same place, same job, day after day. One payday after they found out I was college kid, one of the guys came to me with his check.

"Could you tell me what this says?"

"Yeah, see, it says right here. Social Security tax."

His face registered confusion. It took me a moment to realize he couldn't read and I stammered trying to hide my shock. How could this be, I thought, that a man who'd worked hard for years to raise a family and give his kids a better life was unable to read his own paycheck?

Some of my coworkers sort of took me under their wings and, contrary to my grandmothers' urging me to set aside my educational goals, lobbied me to stick with it. Their missed opportunities became their aspirations for me.

"Lemme give you some advice, kid," was the usual opening. "Get outta here. Don't make the same mistake the rest of us did. You're better than this."

I flinched when I heard that. I wasn't better. I was just lucky. That anyone felt, on my account, that they had to apologize for how they earned an honest living just wasn't right.

Looking back, I grew up with one foot in each of two distinct worlds. My emotional roots were the members of my family—solidly blue-collar, culturally traditional, frugal to a fault, and still in the process of assimilating. My intellectual roots were all the experiences I had, watching and listening to my father, learning about human nature, how government works, and the art of politics and persuasion.

As I began my investment banking career nearly thirty years ago, I had that same sense of bifurcation. I had one foot in the rarefied atmosphere of an aggressive, storied Wall Street firm. The other was rooted in my blue-collar, immigrant, public service heritage. Although I was inside the bubble, I would always feel I was on the outside looking in.

CHAPTER 2:
NO CLUE

"You have no fucking idea where you're interviewing, do you?"

The guy with the window office overlooking New York Harbor, the Harvard diploma on the wall, the Exeter coffee mug, the Tiffany-framed photos of his family and another of his two Great Danes staring at me, leaned back in his leather executive chair and hooked his thumbs under his suspenders. He squinted at me as if trying to decide, Is this a prank? Is this guy crazy or just ridiculously naive? Why am I talking to this bozo?

My ears blazed with confused humiliation. One of the questions candidates usually asked when interviewing for jobs with the leading accounting firms was, "How long does it take to make partner?" It's a sign the candidate is looking to make a commitment, a good thing.

But when I asked that question at one of the dozen-and

-a-half interviews I had to sit through in order to get hired by Goldman Sachs, the reaction sucked all the air out of the room. "You have no idea where you're interviewing, do you?"

I thought I did. But I would look back later and realize just how clueless I was about the ways of Wall Street in general and about Goldman Sachs in particular. Up until that time I had worked as a management consultant and an accountant with a Big Eight accounting firm. That was sandlot football and this was the major league. It was as if I were interviewing to be a batboy for the New York Yankees and asking how long it would take for me to play on the team.

Goldman was, in fact, the New York Yankees of Wall Street. It was the largest private partnership in the securities business at that time. Goldman was then 115 years old, a cult of ambition, prestige, connections, intelligence, and wealth. The firm employed 7,500 people, of which 5,000 had MBAs. There were fewer than 150 partners at the time. It took a decade or more to even be considered. You had to have demonstrated that you could generate substantial profits for the partnership and that all your loyalties were exclusively to the firm. Kind of like the Mafia, you had to be "made."

And, like the Mafia, those who had made partner stayed there. To leave for better money was "not acceptable," according to former partner Steven G. Mandis. In his 2013 book, *What Happened To Goldman Sachs*, Mandis said a partner who left for better money "might send the message that money is the primary driver."

> If the reason for leaving is that the partner no longer enjoys the work, then people would wonder what there is about Goldman not to like. The firm convinces people

that just being a Goldman employee, let alone a partner, is something one would never want to surrender— social identification, prestige, money, and access, and it is perceived as serving a higher good. So if a partner leaves, something has to be wrong with him, and the firm perpetuates that belief through whispers.

Fortunately, the job I was initially hired for—a new "early warning" trading-risk assessment team they were setting up—required neither blind ambition nor a lust for prestige and wealth. It required a calm, pliable demeanor, especially for lower-caste associates like myself. We were expected to defer to the high priests on the trading desk as we begged for a few morsels of information to explain suspect trades.

The team was conceived by several senior partners whose personal wealth was on the line. When a trade went bad— called a "fail to deliver" or a "fail to receive"—they wanted to know what happened and how to keep it from happening again. Profanity, or at least not being offended by it, was helpful.

A twisted sense of humor was definitely an asset in the decade of *Truly Tasteless Jokes*, a series of best-selling paperbacks full of politically incorrect humor. Over-the-top racist, anti-Semitic, homophobic, misogynistic—you name it, nothing was sacred, especially in New York where a young Howard Stern had a new radio show that pushed every button and tested every boundary of decency.

You wouldn't dare tell jokes like that in the workplace today, but at the time the books, jokes, and humor were a huge hit, especially on Wall Street trading desks which were almost uniformly white and male. When the space shuttle *Challenger* exploded during its initial ascent in 1986, it was only minutes before Wall Street was abuzz with freshly minted sick jokes. What does NASA stand for? Need Another Seven Astronauts. Twisted humor has long been Wall Street's way of shedding stress.

One of the early requirements before going into public finance at Goldman was to solve what they called the Polish Lottery question, a kind of moronic joke for finance nerds. "Congratulations! You've won the Polish Lottery. You get a million dollars—to be paid a dollar a year for a million years. How much is that worth today?"

It's a math question—a net present value calculation. Assuming a relatively constant rate of inflation, the dollar you'd get in a hundred years might have the buying power of a few pennies at today's prices. In two hundred years, a dollar will be worthless, especially to the dead-and-buried winner of the Polish Lottery.

The net present value equation is the total amount that a series of future payments is worth today. It is often used as a benchmark for refunding savings or to value assets and investments based on expected future revenue, like bond interest payments. When an investor buys stocks, bonds, or a business, he or she is said to be buying future cash flow at a discount for risks such as inflation, lost opportunity cost, and economic disruption.

When lottery winners take a lump sum payment, the amount is roughly the discounted present value of all the installments that would have been made by taking the money a year at a time. If you won a $10 million lottery today, you'd be offered payments over two or three decades that would equal the $10 million. Or, you could take an immediate lump sum payment that would be a bit less than $6 million, the net present value.

That is a question someone with my education and experience should know how to solve, and I did. The answer in the case of the fake and ridiculous Polish Lottery is that a million dollars paid out at a dollar a year has a present value of a little more than $20.

My college and work experience up to the point when I applied to Goldman Sachs had been far afield of Wall Street's fast-money culture, wood-paneled hallways, brass fittings, and expensive artworks on the walls. After my first two years goofing off at Penn State, I managed to turn my grades around and graduated with a respectable cumulative average—good enough to get me into a top-ranked Master of Science in Management program at Carnegie Mellon in Pittsburgh.

Getting my master's in management turned out to be a smart move, although at the time master's programs in general had been struggling due to the lingering effects of the protracted recession during the 1970s and early 1980s. A 1985 article in the *Wall Street Journal* noted that "some educators say that as many as 25% of the nation's 600 business schools may be forced to close because of the shrinking pool of applicants."

That prediction would turn out to be dead wrong as the trend soon reversed. MBA enrollments, about 60,000 in the US at the time, began surging as the economy took off, entrepreneurship became a hot topic, and Wall Street (thanks in part to films like *Wall Street*, which introduced the concept that in a capitalistic system "greed is good") captured the imaginations of millions of college students. Today some 200,000 people are granted MBA degrees each year.

Through my godfather, Jack Flynn, I applied for and landed an internship the summer between my second and third years at Penn State, at the New Jersey Office of Economic Policy. The offices were across the street from the state capitol in Trenton, a short commute from my parents' home in Levittown. My time was spent crunching numbers for some very smart economists from Princeton and Rutgers who were researching and analyzing the impact gambling was going to have on Atlantic City and the state's economy.

In the 1970s, after fierce debate and political fighting, New Jersey had become the first state outside of Nevada to embrace casino gambling as a "painless" fix (no new taxes to have to sell to the public) for a dilapidated, crime-ridden city and a boost for a state struggling at the time with a stagnant economy. It was also pitched as a way to take a bite out of organized crime in a state that was a Mafia hub and would later inspire television series like *The Sopranos* and *Boardwalk Empire*.

The first casino, Resorts International, had opened just six years earlier, heralded with glowing predictions about how good casinos would be for the beaten-down city and for the state's coffers. When I was hired, the experts were trying to quantify the actual multiplier effect all that hiring of dealers, bartenders, maids, and maintenance workers was having on housing, retail sales, public services, healthcare, tax revenue, and infrastructure.

Analyzing economic input/output models—my first desk

job—was fascinating and I was treated as a membe
team that was grunting it out. The academics were k
who took the time to teach me some tricks of the tr.... a..u
to debate the merits and flaws in econometric models.

One of the most important things policymakers and
regulators wanted to know was how many licenses Atlantic
City could support before the gaming companies would
begin cannibalizing each other's businesses. By the time the
Great Meltdown of 2008 hit, when poker had become a huge
television—and therefore casino—phenomenon, the city
hummed with about a dozen profitable operations.

For many years the casino economy added billions to
the state's purse. But it didn't do much for Atlantic City's
quality of life nor did it make much of a dent in crime and
corruption. If anything, all that cash moving through the
local economy and public institutions was too juicy a quarry
to pass up.

The casino industry played a supporting role in a major
public corruption scandal (code-named Abscam) in the
1970s that sent a busload of elected officials to jail, including
a US Senator, Harrison Williams. Over the years, numerous
city officials—including three mayors—and a bunch of
state officials have been caught, indicted, and convicted of
casino-related corruption.

Out of two hundred US cities, a 2014 Forbes survey ranked
Atlantic City the worst of them all for doing business. An
Atlantic magazine article the same year declared the quality
of life for its citizens was so bad the city "still has trouble
sustaining even a single grocery store."

By 2015, only about seven profitable casinos remained

after four went belly up or closed. The Great Recession wiped out the extra cash that busloads of little old ladies and retirees had been feeding the highly profitable slot machines. Meanwhile, desperate policymakers across the country were climbing on the gambling bandwagon. Competing casinos popped up all over, including just an hour away by car in Philadelphia.

Why is any of this important? That exposure to the mechanics of government finance was the crucible in which my life's work took shape. For a nerdy young wonk who'd spent his childhood sitting in meeting or caucus rooms while his dad debated similar public policy issues, my internship opened a door to an exciting and meaningful career path. It might not pay as well as the corporate world, but it was a profession doing something that mattered to me. It didn't require me to suffer through elections for public office, nor did it require me to kiss a legislative district's worth of constituents. There was no Kissing Mark inside me begging to be let loose.

So that's when I knew I would become a private sector consultant to the public sector. I was still a dreamer. While it might be exciting to work exclusively in the private sector, maybe build and sell a company, or work my way up the ladder to become a corporate executive at a publicly traded company and make sacks of money, for me the public sector was a universe where angelic choirs serenaded noble people who were deciding important issues that would improve life in their communities and the country. I had been raised by a blue-collar defender of the working class who spent his career helping others. I had found a way to follow in his steps and maybe leave a similar footprint.

The New Jersey Office of Economic Policy was two doors away from a beautifully restored Victorian mansion that was the Trenton office of Touche Ross & Co., where my mother was the office manager. Firms like Touche did big business with governments and public authorities, so this office in a major state capital enjoyed some prestige. I'd visit her just about every day, delivering soda during my lunch break. She proudly introduced me to the people she worked for, especially the partners and senior consultants. As a political spouse, my mother was always covering the angles. She was like a mother cheetah on her perch, constantly scanning the horizon for threats and opportunities.

The people who had the sexiest jobs at Touche were the combination CPA/management consultants. They weren't just MBAs and they weren't just auditors. They got their CPA certificates to give them the foundation of accounting and financial forecasting on which their feasibility studies rested. To do that work, I realized, I needed to become a CPA. So in addition to my master's curriculum at Carnegie Mellon, I took accounting courses at Pitt to get the requisite number of credits so that I could start at Touche, sit for the CPA exam, put in a year on the audit staff, and then go into management consulting.

I spent the summer after earning my Masters in a CPA exam prep school with other Touche Ross new hires. It shocked me to discover that almost all of them already had solid plans to leave the firm in two years to open their own offices or join a smaller CPA firm. It seemed bizarre to me that people my age and younger, who hadn't even started their first jobs, were planning their exits and just punching a clock in the meantime to get work experience on their resumes and fulfill the requirements to become a CPA.

What got my blood coursing was not the idea of sitting in some suburban office complex in New Jersey doing routine CPA work for small companies and wealthy families. It was, for example, being involved in feasibility studies for refinancing and reconfiguring the structure, ownership, and management of the sprawling Meadowlands Sports Complex, just across the Hudson River from Manhattan.

I had a management consulting internship at Touche Ross the summer between my two years at Carnegie Mellon and they included me on the team. The proposal was for a new entity, the New Jersey Sports and Exposition Authority, to issue municipal bonds to build a Major League Baseball stadium in the Meadowlands complex. The feasibility study was to show where the revenue would come from to get the bonds paid off.

By the time the bond issue went before the voters in November 1987, just a few weeks after a historic stock market crash, it had become a major political controversy. Proponents claimed it would add more than $100 million to the state's overall economy. Opponents called it a boondoggle at a time when social services and infrastructure needs were more pressing. The amount to be raised—$185 million—was well short of what it was expected to cost. It was hard to believe that the Philadelphia–New York market, with three MLB teams already, could support a fourth starting out with no history or fan base. The voters rejected the issue two to one, probably the right decision. Either way, being part of

24

that process was professional catnip.

So I was delighted when Touche Ross offered me my first real job in their healthcare consulting group, working on feasibility studies for hospitals that were expanding by buying nursing homes and building medical office buildings. Touche Ross felt like home and I was content for the next couple of years. But when someone I worked with went on to Goldman Sachs—making a whole lot more money—and asked me to join him, my head was turned.

That was a big sliding door moment for me, as in the "road not taken" narrative of the 1998 film *Sliding Doors*. The story wove together parallel plotlines for the main character, played by Gwyneth Paltrow. One was her life as it would have been had she gotten onto a subway train just before the sliding doors closed, the other assuming she missed the train.

I'd heard of Goldman Sachs, but Wall Street was a foreign and far away place from my Levittown roots. I went to the library and found a 1983 article in *New York* magazine headlined "Nice Guys Finish First." Rereading it today, it was an over-the-top PR puff piece without a single caveat.

Had I been more experienced, I might have looked at it with a more jaundiced eye. But I wasn't experienced and figured I was a nice-enough guy and had an abundance of self-confidence to work at a firm like that. It sounded like the best possible place in the world for me.

How could I resist a description like this:

> What impresses even Goldman's rivals ... is the firm's across-the-board consistency and excellence in investment banking, block trading, mergers and

acquisitions, risk arbitrage, brokerage research, and several other areas. "We believe in quality, not quantity," says Leon Cooperman, head of Goldman's investment policy committee. ... Best estimates suggest that the firm will earn its partners between $300 million and $400 million in 1983 on revenues of over $1 billion. ... Goldman takes special pride in its renowned equity trading department, perhaps the best operation of its kind on Wall Street. The firm just moved into a new headquarters building at 85 Broad Street which cost $150 million to build.

It sounded like a fairy tale world, an only-in-America success story. Goldman Sachs had been founded in 1869 by Marcus Goldman, a Jewish immigrant from Bavaria who started out—as many German-speaking Jewish immigrants did in those days—as a pushcart peddler.

The two partners in charge at the time were John Whitehead and John Weinberg. One was a Republican and the other a Democrat. Weinberg's father, Sidney, had started out at Goldman in 1907 as a porter's assistant, cleaning toilets and mopping floors. Sidney had climbed the ladder to the top, building up the business and cementing the firm's reputation.

That all sounded so cool. Who wouldn't want to work at a place that even an executive at a competing firm was quoted saying, "It's the class act on Wall Street. What's also amazing is that nearly everyone there is nice."

As I was going through the interview process at Goldman for a job in a newly formed early warning financial and trading monitoring group, I was stunned when one of those nice people laughed at me and said, "You have no fucking idea where you're interviewing, do you?"

CHAPTER 3:
LONG-TERM GREEDY

The year I began my investment banking career, 1987, turned out to be an important inflection point in Wall Street history. The floor of the New York Stock Exchange was still the mob of seething suits, baying voices, and frantic gestures it had been since it was built. Computers were just beginning to play a noticeable role in stock and bond trading.

Three decades later, the old way of doing business seems as quaint as hand-pumping water. The "Big Board," as it used to be called, is practically a living history museum. Jeremy Olshan, editor of MarketWatch, wrote an obituary in 2014 in which he said the only things being exchanged on the floor now are, "camera flashes, sound bites, and [IPO] high-fives."

The action today is inside supercomputers scattered to the four corners of the Earth, handling trades at the speed of light. Between 1987 and now, bit by bit the human touch has succumbed to online and automated trading, quantitative analysis, and financial engineering—big words that make it sound like everything is well-organized and predictable. There were a lot of factors at work in the 2008 market collapse, but behind them all was the steady erosion of personal responsibility. I know because over the years I saw it wash away.

Happily for me, the personal touch was still important in April of 1987, especially at Goldman. I survived all the interviews with various partners and managers to determine if I was a good "cultural fit." The firm took me on at the breathtaking (for me and everybody I had ever known) salary of about $60,000 a year. The national median household income that year, as reported by the Census Bureau, was $25,000.

The rent for our fifth-floor, two-story apartment with a rooftop deck on Manhattan's Upper West Side was $1,900 a month ($5,000+ today), and the average price of a new car was about $10,000 ($35,000 now). When I got my first monthly paycheck I thought there must have been a bookkeeping error.

Just twenty-seven years old, I was suddenly earning about four times what my coworkers at the pulp processing plant had been paid and twice what my steelworker father earned. The money seemed so crazy it would have been embarrassing to talk about, so my wife Diane and I told no one. So much for the long-ago advice of my elders: "This education thing, God knows what you can do with that!"

My principal driver was pride, not money, but soon enough the line between became blurry. I was proud to have made it through the interviews and be able to refer to myself as an investment banker. Of course I was nothing of the sort yet—just one of thousands of newbies who show up each year for their shiny new jobs, excited by the opportunity to play among the big boys and enjoy life at the center of the universe—and terrified of washing out. Just being offered a position at a place like Goldman felt like a personal achievement that conferred residual honor on my tribe. If I survived, it would extend my family's aspirational narrative—the classic immigrant story.

My parents had a vague idea about where I worked but not what I was doing. Their impressions were shaped by the reactions of their friends or acquaintances when they told them that Mark was now working at Goldman Sachs.

"Ohhh! Goldman Saaaachs!"

My father started joking, in mock Italian, that I was a "bigga shotta." He frequently added, "Remember where you came from." Years later, I came to have a deeper appreciation of his message when I read what General George S. Patton said when he was relieved of his command during World War II. It was about the Roman conqueror who returned home in a tumultuous parade while a slave stood behind him, "holding a golden crown, and whispering in his ear a warning—that all glory is fleeting."

The arc of my life now stretched from the kitchen table— where Nana, my Italian grandmother, told me time and again, "Learn a trade!"—to the hallowed halls of Goldman Sachs where the golden rules pounded into our heads were that "the client's interest always comes first," and to think and act "long-term greedy." These two phrases, especially the first, popped up frequently in meetings.

We were to concentrate on creating trust and loyalty

as opposed to just chasing transactions—or so it seemed to me at the time. In such a highly competitive business, a sparkling reputation and fierce customer loyalty is money in the bank and an insurance policy for the partners. The way to maintain and build loyalty, we were repeatedly told, was to always be thinking about the clients' best interests. That's how the firm made money—by being long-term greedy.

So much has been written about the early history, the characters, and the recent past of Goldman Sachs that almost anything I might add about the big picture would be superfluous. Some excellent books whose titles seem to sum it up include: *Money And Power: How Goldman Sachs Came To Rule The World*, by William D. Cohan; and *What Happened To Goldman Sachs: An Insider's Story of Organizational Drift and Its Unintended Consequences*, by Steven G. Mandis. Put those two together and you've got a fairly accurate thumbnail profile.

You could say there have always been two Goldman Sachs, and that the firm has always been disciplined about differentiating between them. Cohan, a journalist who became an investment banker, wrote in his book that, "From the outside, Goldman Sachs is the perfect company ... smarter, more ethical, and more profitable than all of its competitors. Behind closed doors, the firm constantly straddles the line between conflict of interest and legitimate deal making."

That was the criticism levelled against Goldman after the financial market meltdown in 2008. An internal email surfaced that described a collateralized debt obligation (CDO) the firm was underwriting as "a shitty deal."

Recognizing that the whole CDO market was on the brink of collapse, the firm—while continuing to offer the "shitty" CDOs to customers—made a huge bet with its own principal that paid off in the billions when CDOs finally did go into the crapper.

There's no way to camouflage such self-interest, even for Goldman Sachs. Grilled about it by a Senate investigations committee in 2010, CEO Lloyd Blankfein tried and failed to talk his way around it. Clients, he said, "are not coming to us to represent what our views are. ... [T]he nature of the principal business in market making is that we are the other side of what our clients want to do."

That's double-talk for, Hey, if customers want to buy our shitty CDOs, who are we to say they shouldn't? It's a free country, right? And don't we have a duty to our shareholders to protect their investment and make as much profit as possible? So, where's the problem?

Cohan says the other Goldman Sachs, the "perfect" one, was the only large Wall Street firm in 2008 that refused on principle to host a fundraiser for Rudolph Giuliani's presidential bid. The seeds of that refusal had been planted twenty years earlier at the dawn of my career.

Giuliani was the US Attorney in New York before he was elected mayor. He had launched a legally flawed but politically inspired campaign to put a bunch of Wall Street executives in jail for insider trading. He held press conferences on the steps of the federal courthouse in Manhattan and railed against "Wall Street greed," promising that fighting white-collar crime would be a new priority. He promised to break up the mob of Rolex-wearing thieves that was supposedly cheating America's hard-working "little-guy" investors.

His tactics included carefully staged daytime raids on Wall Street offices, with news outlets tipped in advance. The result was provocative footage of investment bankers in Armani suits being perp-walked down the street in Guccis and handcuffs. Those images horrified everyone in the banking business. Such public shaming had always been reserved for when the good guys caught a Ponzi schemer about to flee the country, or they shut down a penny stock boiler room.

Many of the people arrested in Giuliani's war were longtime bankers and civic leaders whose names and brand affiliations guaranteed front-page coverage. The public loved the crusade but many of the cases that resulted in charges being filed proved to be weak or legally convoluted. The only way Giuliani could win convictions was by bullying defendants into taking pleas to avoid being tied up in court, hemorrhaging legal fees. It was high theater and low blows, and it worked.

The resulting storm of publicity boosted Giuliani's lawman credentials and polished his tin star. That served his political ambitions but made him a leper on Wall Street. He had the shrewd instinct to bail while he was ahead. In the middle of prosecuting a half-dozen major cases touching on important constitutional issues, before any inconvenient legal setbacks could stain his tough-guy rep, Rudy quit his crime crusade, packed up his press clippings, and rode off to launch his bid for mayor.

A number of the major cases he initiated ended up falling apart. None produced the mother of all indictments he'd hinted was coming. Twenty years later, when he was running for president, the names of the guilty as well as the innocent had long since faded from memory. In the interim he'd had a good eight-year run as New York's feisty mayor and then reinvented himself after September 11 as a civilian war hero. As for his aborted campaign to clean up Wall Street, the dogs had barked and the caravan had moved on.

Except at Goldman Sachs. One of those whom Rudy had targeted was a senior Goldman partner, Robert M. Freeman. Pundits would later say Freeman was either "the victim of a witch hunt" or "a guilty bystander to insider trading." Whichever it was, Freeman took a plea deal and served four months in prison. His decision to throw himself on Giuliani's grenade saved the firm and his fellow partners from a long-drawn-out legal battle and a never-ending public relations disaster.

Two decades later, Giuliani's money people were baffled by Goldman's refusal to host a fundraiser. All the other big firms were doing one. Can't bygones be bygones? Cohan wrote in his book that a Goldman partner replied, "You do not understand. It is the Goldman Sachs DNA."

CHAPTER 4:
CHIMPS IN T-SHIRTS

"Who the hell do you think you are?"

A senior Goldman partner who ran the municipal bond department had just popped his cork at a monthly department meeting and was lecturing a group of bankers who were grumbling about their bonuses. It was early in 1988, just a couple of months after Black Monday, October 19, 1987, when the bottom fell out of the stock market. The Dow Jones Industrial Average lost nearly a quarter of its value in one trading session, a percentage record that still stands.

In retrospect, the market was due for a correction after posting a one-year gain of nearly 45 percent that August. Collapsing oil prices and tension in the Middle East helped set the stage, weakening stock prices in the days leading up to Black Monday. The catalyst for the sudden one-day downdraft was said to be "program trading," the term used at the time to describe trading decisions dictated by complex new computing programs—algorithms—that were supposed to be more precise and faster than the humans they replaced. These automated number crunchers were being widely used to run portfolio strategies for hedging risk.

When prices started to plunge in earnest on Black Monday, the swoon triggered a cascade of computer-driven sell orders that drove prices lower yet, triggering more sell orders, and so on. The rout went global and in the weeks that followed many economists were predicting a 1930s-style economic cataclysm.

The lecture I witnessed took place early in 1988, during one of my first monthly department meetings as a new kid. Attendance was mandatory and everyone was expected to be there on time. At the stroke of 8:00 a.m., the heavy walnut doors to the meeting room were closed and locked. No one dared leave. If you were just fifteen seconds late, you were locked out of the entire meeting and would have to ask people to tell you what happened. Having spent as many hours as I had watching government in action, I was impressed by the discipline and determined to never get locked out.

The meetings were held in a large room in Goldman's offices that was paneled in dark woods and classically tricked out with chandeliers, original paintings by name-brand artists, oriental rugs—the works. No matter how minor one's role in the firm, or how small the desk, in that cocoon of privilege and prosperity you could easily imagine yourself a member of an exclusive club. It was effective theater—what sane person wouldn't work his butt off to remain a member?

At that meeting, the partner who headed the department was leading a scripted discussion when several of the eighty or so bankers began nudging it off agenda. They were mumbling and grousing that their compensation was light compared with their contributions to the department's profits. They thought they deserved more—much more. The banter escalated until the partner, his face flush, finally lost it.

"Who the hell do you think you are? Listen, I could take a chimp, put a Goldman Sachs T-shirt on the chimp, send the chimp out there, and the chimp would do really well for itself."

I had yet to learn what people were being paid, or why the partner was so upset. I had no way of judging the merits of anyone's argument. But it left the indelible impression that the institution always comes before the individual. It was a jolt of reality because it's true. When clients spoke of their bankers' recommendations to their trustees, they didn't invoke the name of their contact at Goldman Sachs. They just said, "Goldman Sachs recommends ..." Any warm, fuzzy ideas I still had about the dharma of investment banking were drowned that day like a sack of kittens.

The message was clear. Bankers who raise the money to make big dreams come true may think they "hung the moon," but it was the Goldman Sachs brand that made the difference. We bankers were cannon fodder—expendable and replaceable commodities.

The reaction of the assembled bankers to this tirade about chimps in T-shirts was predictably defiant. I would discover in time that we bankers have a tendency toward mood swings, between supreme confidence and pathetic insecurity. That's the personality profile of an investment banker—someone who needs a steady flow of praise to keep from becoming a basket case.

Because Wall Street as an institution is the only business where people who are not entrepreneurs can become crazy rich, it attracts the most competitive people. They all have the same goal—get the biggest possible slice of pie. They worked the hardest and played the roughest.

In spite of the partner's tirade—a sobering orientation—Goldman Sachs turned out to be the perfect place for me to learn how to become a great banker. I was the diligent, bag-carrying associate for a dozen seasoned healthcare VPs. I learned something from each of them—what to emulate and what not—that stuck to me like pollen to a bee.

It was my good luck that I didn't land at any of our competitors at the time, among them Salomon Brothers, First Boston, Paine Webber, Lehman Brothers, Drexel Burnham Lambert, Donaldson Lufkin & Jenrette, and Bear Stearns. Of that group, Goldman is the sole survivor.

Salomon Brothers, which had been a leader in municipal bonds through the 1980s, shocked Wall Street by exiting municipal finance after passage of the Tax Reform Act of 1986. The new law made tax-exempt bonds less competitive and curbed the interest deduction on money borrowed to buy municipals.

Salomon got into trouble in 1991 for manipulating treasury bond prices. The firm had to pay out several hundred million in fines, was absorbed by Travelers Group, and served as the inspiration for Tom Wolfe's 1987 Wall Street satire *The Bonfire of the Vanities* as well as Michael Lewis's 1989 insider tell-all, *Liar's Poker*. Citigroup acquired the brand as part of a merger and in 2003, after a fresh wave of scandals, quietly buried the remains.

Paine Webber was 120 years old in 2000 and in good health when the firm's principal partner and longtime guiding hand decided to sell it to UBS, the Swiss mega-bank, where it was eventually digested and the brand put out to pasture. UBS has been at the center of several major scandals, from Long-Term Capital in 1998 to the global interest rate-manipulation case known as the Libor scandal (London Interbank Offered Rate). UBS abandoned municipal bonds in 2008.

First Boston, whose founders had revolutionized the way public companies were bought and sold, became insolvent in 1989 when the junk bond market collapsed. The firm had made a heavy investment in the bonds of a mattress company and had to be rescued. Then it became part of a larger bank, Credit Suisse, that had its own scandals to answer for. The firm closed down its municipal finance department in 1995. The First Boston name was put out of its misery in 2006.

Merrill Lynch & Co., the world-famous "thundering herd" retail brand founded in 1914, got into trouble in 1994 and had to shell out nearly half a billion dollars after its public finance department was accused of knowingly selling risky investments to Orange County, California. Those investments contributed to the county becoming one of history's largest municipal bankruptcies, a rarity in any size, and easily its most embarrassing—it turned out that the Orange County treasurer's financial advisors included a mail-order astrologer and a psychic.

Merrill got into big trouble again in 2002 for publishing misleading stock research, and then again in 2008 during the financial crisis. The firm was accused of misrepresenting the risks associated with those toxic mortgage-backed securities that wrecked the economy. By the time the dust had settled, Merrill had been mopped up and become part of Bank of America, which has had its own plateful of scandals and controversies. Unlike many of its brethren, it has managed to survive.

Lehman Brothers, founded in 1850—nineteen years before Goldman Sachs—had survived all that time to become the fourth-largest investment bank in the US— until September 2008 when it went bankrupt. The firm was brought down almost overnight by its too-big bet on subprime mortgage-backed securities. The collapse exposed sketchy practices and what one report described as "no accountability for failure." Barclays Bank had the honor of scraping Lehman's carcass off the pavement and, like Drexel Burnham Lambert, the brand became a symbol of Wall Street excess at its most wretched.

Bear Stearns was the youngest and scrappiest of the group, a firm noted for making highly leveraged bets but also named the "Most Admired" securities firm in a *Fortune* magazine survey three years in a row. Bear Stearns had bet heavily on asset-backed securities and got caught with its pants down. In 2008 I was working at JPMorgan Chase when Bear Stearns was absorbed into our firm. I was assigned the unpleasant task of unemploying more than 150 bankers on both teams who had either become redundant or were too distinct and unconnected to the more profitable mainstream sectors.

Goldman had a particular aura about it that was hard to describe but was real to those who worked there. Ethnically the firm skewed toward its Jewish roots, with a large Italian-American contingent in operations, a team of Ivy Leaguers in investment banking, and a battalion of ex-military in mergers and acquisitions.

It was the most Democrat-leaning bank, tended to support government and public-sector causes, and many of its alumni did stints in highly visible government roles, like Treasury Secretaries Robert Rubin and Henry Paulson. From where I sat, it was the most public-spirited firm on the Street, and many of its senior partners were authentically altruistic, all of which was good for business. It was long-term greedy.

From the start I learned that the stereotype of the young investment banker chained to his desk until midnight is accurate. It was like moving to a foreign country and having to learn a new job while learning a new language—arduous, nerve-racking, time-consuming but exciting.

Late one Friday, after many nights in a row getting home with just enough time to eat and sleep, I was feeling sorry for myself as I slouched into the elevator. It was after 11 o'clock, a quiet time in the building. Everyone else had gone home. That district of the city goes dormant at night and on weekends. I was feeling guilty that once again I'd let work take precedence over an evening out.

On its descent to the lobby, the car jolted to a stop at the eleventh floor, the executive suite, and the doors opened to admit a guy in a suit carrying a huge, unwieldy stack of documents and binders under each arm. I immediately recognized Bob Rubin, then co-chairman of the Goldman board and, among other activities, a board member of New York's Mount Sinai Hospital, a client and one of the oldest and largest teaching hospitals in the US.

Whether that mountain of paper he seemed to be in danger of dropping was for Goldman or Mount Sinai, I was impressed that a guy in his position was schlepping his own work home so late at night, on a weekend, no less. It fit the image I had of the firm as relatively down to earth—as down to earth as Wall Street gets, anyway.

Being compared to chimps had been a little deflating but those I worked with on the public finance side knew they were instrumental and thought well enough of themselves as do-gooders that the criticism lacked real bite. On a day when our colleagues on the corporate side might be congratulating themselves on a huge IPO that made them and the firm a pile of money, members of the public finance department's healthcare group might be celebrating the successful sale of bonds to build a new heart center.

Many of us, myself included, believed our efforts resulted in the proverbial win-win. We made money for the firm and helped finance healthcare for the public. As far as the partnership and the firm was concerned, however, we were ringing up nickels and dimes compared to the metaphorical bricks of hundred-dollar bills brought in by our corporate counterparts.

Public finance is the Rodney Dangerfield of investment banking—it gets very little respect. When I was sent to recruiting events at the nation's top MBA schools, I'd inevitably find myself in a quiet corner of the room talking to the occasional nerd while a throng of short-term greedy students buzzed around the mergers and acquisitions (M&A) bankers.

Unlike the kids clamoring to get on the Wall Street bandwagon and make a killing, people who choose careers in public finance are more interested in making a living. They want to do good while doing great for themselves. I shared that feeling, although in my case public finance chose me.

Originally I was hired to work with a new risk monitoring group at Goldman, a job for which I was well-qualified—a CPA with a background in financial analysis, forecasting, and econometrics. Public finance was a good match for a guy who'd grown up around politicians and civil servants. Less than a year after I started at Goldman, a partner who'd interviewed me and who, like me, had grown up in the Philadelphia area and had attended the local Catholic schools, drafted me into public finance.

It was a perfect fit. Bankers in public finance are essentially brand marketers who go out across the country to call on state and local governments, airports, housing and transportation authorities, universities, and hospitals. The primary service they offer is facilitating the sale of municipal bonds on behalf of public and quasi-public entities that need to raise money to build or acquire infrastructure and to refinance existing debt. The clients tend to be congenial and there is a sense of shared interest in the outcome—a new dormitory, upgrading a worn-out sewage system, modernizing an airport to make it safer.

Corporate investment bankers have a menu of services they can offer to big international companies in every conceivable line of business—big-picture stuff like mergers, underwriting stock and bond offerings, leveraged finance, and hedging risk on interest rates, currencies, and commodities. For every dollar of profit generated by public finance, the corporate side earned many multiples.

In contrast to governmental entities like cities and

states, healthcare and higher education clients are typically represented by their chief financial officers and treasurers. Whereas municipal borrowers usually have to put out a request for proposals for a bond issue or solicit competitive bids, with universities and hospital systems it's more of a corporate relationship business. For years those borrowers tended to lock themselves up with one investment bank, which is why brand reputation and client service are keys to success.

Depending on the state of the credit markets and other factors, bankers like myself would present our firm's best ideas for refinancing debt or how we would price municipal bonds at the lowest cost of capital. One of the deals I worked on, for example, was funding a new football stadium for the University of Notre Dame. A Goldman partner sat on Notre Dame's board, which had everything to do with why we got the business. That sort of thing was typical and Goldman was especially assertive about getting its partners on the boards of coveted public finance clients.

The process was subtle, as opposed to an overt ask. But partners would flex a little muscle now and then when it could do the firm some good. I know of one Goldman partner who heard we were pitching his alma mater, to which he had donated millions of dollars over the years. He immediately picked up the phone and had his secretary get the president of the university on the phone. After the initial pleasantries, the partner blurted, "You know, Goldman Sachs has been good to the university so I'm confident the university will be good to Goldman Sachs."

For hospitals and universities, one of the core profitable

strategies for many years was arbitraging interest rates, although we avoided talking about it in those terms. From a peak in the 1980s, interest rates began a decades-long decline that generated a lot of business. A university with a fat endowment fund earning 8 percent or more didn't want to spend that money for a new stadium when it could borrow at 5 percent and pocket the difference, tax-free.

That was a dominant part of the municipal finance business in those years for all the Wall Street investment banks. We aided and abetted tax-avoidance arbitrage plays for not-for-profit hospitals and universities.

Because municipal bond interest income is exempt from taxes, the IRS has the authority to raise a red flag if it thinks an institution is getting too aggressive. The avoided taxes cost the federal Treasury. But it was considered a legitimate strategy and more palatable considering the purpose—better healthcare. Besides, there is no rule or law that forces an institution, public or private, to deplete its cash and investments before issuing debt.

One of the reasons I enjoyed working in public finance is that municipal clients are essentially permanent institutions whereas companies like Google and Facebook, which have been public companies for only a few years, may not be around a decade from now. In 2005, Blockbuster Video had 10,000 stores and Myspace was the world's largest social networking website. Eight years later Blockbuster was defunct and Myspace was the punchline for a joke. Similarly, corporate investment bankers are always in demand, wooed away by competing banks, becoming corporate treasurers and CFOs, or joining private equity groups and hedge funds.

Institutions like Massachusetts General Hospital, Cleveland Clinic, and the University of Chicago, some of which have been around for more than a century, will most likely be around a hundred years from now. As for personnel, in municipals we used to joke that no one ever leaves the business. I've met plenty of people in their sixties and seventies who had been public finance bankers their entire lives, working with the same clients their entire careers. That began to change in 2008 and a significant number of senior bankers have left public finance in the years since.

At $60,000 a year to start, I had nothing to complain about. When one of the partners handed me my first bonus check, for $40,000, it was like winning the lottery. He must have mistaken my stunned reaction as disappointment because he apologized. "Don't worry. You're going to make a lot more money than this. For now, we're saying we really like what you're doing."

My first year in public finance at Goldman Sachs was a ride through a funhouse of distorted mirrors. I'd stumbled into a profession and a niche within it that was challenging and rewarding. I'd had a front row seat during a year of high drama in the markets. I was earning a great living in a great city. Most importantly, I'd found the love of my life—a beautiful, caring, honest, down-to-earth soulmate—and Diane and I were married.

Not a bad year for a chimp.

CHAPTER 5: SURF 'N' TURF IN STYROFOAM

Is this heaven?

I wondered that as I leafed through the massive binder someone had just dropped on my desk. It was full of elegantly printed menus bearing the names of restaurants I had read about in the *New York Times*—page after page of tantalizing descriptions of dishes at prices to choke on.

There was Harry's at Hanover Square; Indochine (hip French colonial Vietnamese); Chanterelle, which had received a rare four-star review (the lentil soup flavored with ham and truffles sounded good!); Smith & Wollensky, the Vatican of dry-aged steaks; Delmonico's; Dock's Oyster Bar—all legendary names. Every fancy restaurant from Wall Street to Chelsea was represented. And it was all on the company tab, which explained the flimsy Styrofoam takeout containers I'd noticed late at night on other people's desks, often with half-eaten filet mignons and lobster tails.

My first day on the job at Goldman I had been loading spreadsheets and crunching numbers for hours when I took a break and strolled around the offices. It was after normal business hours, except there were no normal business hours in investment banking. Five o'clock had long since come and gone and the people I worked with were glued to their chairs, behaving as if they were never going to go home.

A few had found ways to sneak out unnoticed. One of my cubicle neighbors would microwave a steaming hot cup of coffee, set it on his desk in front of an open spreadsheet on his monitor, leave his desk lamp on, and drape his jacket over his chair. Then he'd leave and everyone thought he was still there.

So I kept working on my assignment as my stomach began to growl. As the new guy I didn't dare leave my post before the others, even to dash down to the street to grab a slice of pizza. I didn't want anyone to see me putting on my jacket or walking to the elevator, but I didn't want to ask a dumb question about finding out the routine. Finally some helpful person at another desk asked if I wanted to order in.

"That'd be great." I imagined spoiling myself with one of those fat delicatessen sandwiches that could only be found in New York—hot corned beef with cole slaw and Russian dressing on thick slices of fresh rye. Instead, this fellow dropped the massive binder of menus on my desk. "Have a look. If you've never had the filet from Delmonico's, it's as good as it gets. Make sure to order it Pittsburgh rare."

At the job I'd just left, at a staid Big Eight accounting firm, if you got hungry and had to work late—seven o'clock was late—you got a modest per diem for takeout or you

THE PRIVATE LIFE OF PUBLIC FINANCE

bought your own meal. So I'd run out and grab a burger and fries or Chinese takeout. Working late at Goldman was late—easily after ten, often until eleven, sometimes later. The firm picked up the tab for late dinners, anything you wanted from any restaurant you fancied. I'm a foodie and it was a kid-in-a-candy-store experience.

Bankers like myself, who put in twelve- to fourteen-hour days, were also given car fare home, Wall Street style. I'd emerge from 85 Broad Street and find a dozen or so black Lincoln Town Cars idling at the curb, any one of which was ready to whisk me home like a potentate. It didn't matter if home was a six-block ride uptown or a sixty-mile trek to suburban New Jersey. The message was clear—you may be a chimp but you're worth more than fast food and grubby subway rides. Hang the expense!

As I would later learn, there was no expense to hang, at least not for Goldman Sachs. The cost of those four-star meals and the limo rides home would find their way into a customer debit, hiding behind some accounting category amorphously labeled "other expenses" under the "components of gross spread."

My friends and family were agog when I told them the stories about my first days. As clear as those first impressions are today, it only took a couple of weeks for me to feel the love and get into the groove. As my investment banking career began, flying first class, staying at the best hotels, and eating like an emperor was intoxicating. After awhile, it was what you expected and felt you deserved because you worked your ass off at the best investment bank in the world. It was a spawning ground for prima donnas and the self-delusional types who imagined themselves as masters of their universes.

The real world—the one where somebody had to crawl under a hot factory oven to clean out drywall debris or swab toilets or swing a sledge—was never too far from my mind. The pampering was nice but deep down I always felt like a spectator, watching a crazy business at a crazy time from a distance.

In those days car services communicated with their dispatchers via open channels on citizen's band (CB) radios. Goldman partners were referred to on the radio as Mr. or Ms. For the rest of us, it was just the last name: Melio at 76th and West End. The ride home would often be punctuated by bursts of scratchy chatter between a dispatcher and other drivers. On my ride home one night during my first summer, the radio crackled to life and the dispatcher hailed another driver with special instructions.

"So-and-So [a colleague] left the city for the weekend and forgot her tennis racket. See the doorman to pick it up and take it out to East Hampton. Stand by for the address."

"Oh my God!" I blurted. "Is that for real?"

"Yes sir," the driver replied. "We get calls like that all the time. Somebody forgets their glasses and needs to get them out to the airport before their flight leaves. One time I drove a guy to a Jets game at the Meadowlands and he had me wait through the whole game and then take him to the airport. I heard he got in a little trouble for that one."

"So somebody is actually going to drive an empty Town Car a hundred miles each way from Manhattan to the end of Long Island—what is it, four hours—just to deliver a tennis racket? That's gotta cost ... what?"

"Two hundred, plus a fifty-dollar surcharge for trips over two hours. Crazy, right?"

There was such profligacy that to earn a reprimand or a footnote in the mythology of wretched excess at Goldman you had to do something that was off the charts. A partner who had already earned a reputation for testing the boundaries found one when—late for his flight back to New York—he pulled up at the departures platform at LAX, grabbed his bag, and abandoned his rental car at the curb.

As he rushed inside the terminal he yelled to a guy at the rental car desk, "Outside. Black something-or-other. Key's in the ignition! It's one of yours!" The next day the rental company reported it stolen.

I happened to arrive at the office the morning two of the managing partners and in-house counsel were giving this other partner holy hell that you could hear all the way from the elevators.

"What the FUCK were you thinking! Our insurance company sure ain't gonna pay a claim for a car you practically invited somebody to rip off."

His defense? "Hey, we made half a million on the deal I did out there! You don't understand—I HAD to make that flight." His emergency? He had a date with Iman, then the hottest model on the planet.

As the months and years at Goldman began to accumulate, long-term greedy took on a second meaning. It still described a firm of partners whose loyal customers trusted us and brought us repeat business year after year. But change was in the air. It was rumored in the media that some partners wanted out and were worried about missing the chance to cash in on the long-term bull market.

It became clear that Goldman Sachs would be joining its competitors by going public. If you're thinking about going public, you want to rack up a few good earnings years first, to brag about and give analysts some rosy data to support a premium stock price.

As the 1990s rolled out, "long-term greedy" started to feel more like "be greedy now."

CHAPTER 6:
TROPHIES AND TOYS

In my early days as the junior guy on the team, I was often responsible for procuring last-minute theater and sports tickets at scalped prices for clients and senior bankers. Every firm had its own system for keeping those expenses off the firm's books. One was through financial printers that produced the offering and other documents associated with securities deals. They wanted our business and were happy to bury those hard-to-explain expenses.

If we needed theater tickets to entertain clients, I was instructed to order the tickets from the printer, who would buy them and build the cost into the bill. If the print job cost $40,000 and they'd laid out $10,000 worth of theater tickets, the printing bill would come in at $50,000. The senior bankers loved the system of getting credit for grand gestures for free and the clients went home bragging about how "our bankers" had the best seats in the house.

The night the offering documents were ready for mailing, junior bankers like myself would be sent to proofread the final copy. If it was a big job, the printer would sometimes put out a lavish spread of food and booze. One had billiards tables, pinball, and the latest video games—Donkey Kong, Galaga, Golden Tee Golf—to keep us occupied after we had finished proofreading and we waited for the job to be finished and loaded into a secure truck.

Among the more frivolous expenses were deal toys. A deal toy is to a banker what a stag's head is to a hunter. Both are proudly displayed in a prominent wall position as evidence of a successful kill. Before the boom that began in the early 1980s, a banker who had worked on a big underwriting would get a framed copy, embedded in Lucite, of what was known as the tombstone—the full-page ad that had appeared in the *Wall Street Journal* announcing the deal and naming the firms in the underwriting syndicate.

By the late 1980s the deal toy had evolved under the influence of all those Ivy Leaguers who'd been hired during the boom. Tombstones became more elaborate, which is about what you'd expect when the guys in a mostly guys-only club like Wall Street find themselves with too much time or money or both on their hands. Instead of a dull display of text, the deal details were engraved on all kinds of objects—sculpture reproductions, briefcases, mini basketball backboards, ping putters, baseball bats, and end tables.

Icon Recognition, the company that made much of this junk, churned out some elaborate deal toys: a gold-plated reproduction of the Mandalay Bay Hotel, including swimming pool; a miniature reproduction of a sculpture of Apollo slaying a bear with bow and arrow; a miniature strummable banjo. Icon's president told a writer from The New Yorker that JPMorgan Chase once ordered Lucite blocks about a foot square with the head of a dinosaur embedded inside. It was for the bankers who'd worked on a deal with Universal, owner of the *Jurassic Park* franchise.

It was common to order one for everyone on the banking team and for the client participants, perhaps thirty at about $300 each—nearly $10,000 spent on vanity trinkets that were destined to end up in a yard sale or a trash bin. The firm picked up the tab, and then promptly passed it on as other expenses.

Most clients never knew, but likely suspected, they were paying for that stuff. It was all rolled up in the deal and only the investment bankers knew how much it cost.

For example, in the mid- to late-1980s, a firm underwriting a $100 million transaction might earn the bankers about $1 million, of which about $200,000 would be management fees, $700,000 in sales commissions (split among sales, trading, and underwriting), and maybe $50,000 would be legitimate itemized underwriter's expenses—legal fees, travel, and such. The last $50,000, an amount small enough to seem trivial, might be listed as "other expenses," and would include the lavish dinners, Town Cars, tickets for ball games and Broadway shows, and deal toys for the masters of the universe.

The foundation of the modern Wall Street ecosystem was being laid down during that time and would play a pivotal role in blowing up our economy two decades later. The 1980s inspired some cultural iconography that's stood the test of time. Oliver Stone's film *Wall Street* gave us the expression

"Greed is good." *Bonfire of the Vanities*, which portrayed an arrogant young bond salesman at Salomon Brothers, was billed as, "An outrageous story of greed, lust and vanity in America." It was the decade of yuppies, BMWs, Robin Leach's *Lifestyles of the Rich and Famous*, Donald Trump's *The Art Of The Deal*, trickle-down economics, gentrification, and the pursuit of "having it all."

Competition from commercial banks in the 1990s began to dampen some of the reckless spending, but the 2008 financial crisis really turned the screws. The stretch limos no longer wait outside New York's most exclusive restaurants, nor do bankers throw themselves lavish dinner celebrations.

At most investment banks today, bankers must submit detailed restaurant receipts, listing who attended and itemizing every menu item ordered. Today's deal toys tend to be small lucite trophies that the bankers have to pay for out of their own pockets.

The hidden cost of self-pampering was one thing, but the pricing of bond deals was a black box. That gave the sales, trading, underwriting, and derivative desks opportunites to make significant amounts of money for the bank without the client's knowledge.

The financial industry got away with that kind of chicanery because the people who sat across the tables from us—directors and executives of non-for-profit hospitals—tended to be community business people and career public servants. To them Wall Street was a giant ball of string. They treated their investment bankers with the sort of deference reserved for doctors. "Okay! You know more about it than I do. I'm sure you know best."

That first part was true. What wasn't true was the implication that we investment bankers were working for them, that we practiced what we had been preached: "Remember, the client's interests always come first. We're building relationships. Let's keep it long-term greedy." We were not doctors and we observed no Hippocratic oath to "First, do no harm."

As I learned how things worked in the real world, my interpretation of long-term greedy began to evolve, closer to William D. Cohan's description in his Goldman history, *Money and Power*. "Behind closed doors, [Goldman Sachs] constantly straddles the line between conflict of interest and legitimate deal making."

The shenanigans were nearly universal. Everybody did it. That's how I came to straddle the line between loyalty to my firm and my sense of moral responsibility to my customers. I could have said something, but that would have raised doubts that I was a team player. Besides, what would I say? That we were making an awful lot of money? That was our job! I didn't know then what I've learned since so I kept my suspicions and instincts to myself.

I had begun my career a blank slate at an old established firm with a well-defined and embedded culture. If it was okay at Goldman to feast at the customer's expense, then it must be standard operating procedure everywhere. Besides, we were encouraged to believe we deserved special status. We were the best and brightest and nobody worked harder.

But even the veterans on the banking side were stunned when we found out, as we did once, that a deal which was projected to earn the firm $1 million turned into a $5 million profit. The swap desk had identified and exploited an opportunity. We all cheered but it felt a little like going to an ATM for $100 and having it shoot hundred-dollar bills at you for five minutes. Caught up in the moment, the distinction between right and wrong became fuzzy.

Any twinge of guilt I may have felt back then was offset by the genuine pleasure I got from the idealistic belief that I was helping hospitals deliver better healthcare to their communities. If I had been a corporate banker I might have been talking to technology companies about semiconductors—possibly interesting, but not for long.

As a public finance banker specializing in not-for-profit healthcare, just about everybody you meet has a dramatic story or two (or three) to tell. It might be an inspirational patient, a health tragedy, a crisis faced, or a disaster averted.

Public finance clients tend to stay in one place a long time and as a banker I got to know many on a personal level—births, graduations, weddings, funerals. When friends face a medical dilemma, I'm often able to refer them, with the help of my clients, to the hospitals and to the doctors who are the most respected among their peers. In spite of the world of not-for-profit hospitals becoming a conglomerated industry, even today the vast majority of people in leadership roles still care, have hearts and consciences, and take personal pride in their successes.

As for the nuts and bolts of pricing and trading, or why Aunt Bertha was sold a hospital bond at a 4 percent yield when they were initially priced to yield 5 percent—none of that showed up on my radar. My banking colleagues and I trusted our brethren on the desks. We never knew how the bonds traded in the secondary market until the last few years when the Municipal Securities Rulemaking Board made this information available. I shudder when I think of some of the things that must have been going on.

All of this was possible to get away with because hospitals that needed to raise capital lacked the knowledge and experience in the financial markets to evaluate deals. If and when they did, they discovered there were no alternatives. The game was essentially rigged by Wall Street for Wall Street in a hundred small ways, not the grand conspiracy that Rudy Giuliani portrayed in the 1980s.

For example, those of us inside the bubble knew that swap transactions were unusually profitable, but we never suspected that certain desks were colluding, that some firms' swap desks would make informal deals with each other to reduce competition. "Hey, how about we'll lay low on the bidding on this one if you'll lay low on the next?"

The typical 1980s trustee at any of the 5,000 or so independent hospitals and health systems in the US was a civic or business leader who had no background in finance, medical care, or hospital management. Boardrooms were largely populated by car dealers, politicians, local bank presidents—people with good intentions and healthy egos. They deserved respect for volunteering their time, but few had much to offer of a debt capital markets nature.

The people running hospitals in the early days were missionary types—typically older men or women who were leaders in their faiths and religious institutions. In the next generation there were a number of management consultants who used a lot of jargon and occasionally had some loopy ideas.

A banker friend who was working at another firm years ago recalls a visit his team paid to a health system in the Midwest. "We had worked up a debt restructuring proposal for the CFO, who had previously been a management consultant. When we finished with the pleasantries, he says, 'We'd like you to work on taking the system public.'

"We all looked at each other with that WTF expression, and then he added, 'We don't want to pay you until it goes public. We'd like to have a relationship where you show me yours and I'll show you mine.'"

Turning a public asset like a public not-for-profit hospital into a Wall Street IPO, enriching the current management in the process, would never pass muster with any state's attorney general. It was such a ludicrous idea that my friend, a junior analyst at the time, was embarrassed just to be in the room.

"But our team leader, a senior guy, was leaning forward, nodding his head, acting like he was really interested. When the CFO finished a monologue that was hard to follow as well as insulting, our lead banker says, 'You know what, this is so forward thinking and visionary that we'd like a chance to go back and see how we can respond. We need some time.'

"When we were safely out of earshot, the rest of us were all over the senior guy. 'What the hell were you doing, nodding like that?'

"He said, 'I had no fucking idea what that guy was talking about. I just wanted to get the hell out of there.' We never heard from them again."

Today, a new generation has taken over and the vast majority of people in top management are professional health administrators and/or finance, accounting, tax, and compliance experts.

It was my job to help manage client relationships. I learned to be alert for bankers who weren't paying attention. In general, bankers love to talk, so they tend to be lousy listeners.

Once, for a meeting with the CFO of a western US hospital system, we arranged to fly in some of our experts on structured products from New York. The CFO was a former banker himself and he didn't say much as he sat there while our people described with ginned-up enthusiasm whatever new and improved financial pretzel they were pitching but vaguely understood. These were known as "proprietary" products—ingenious, unique, and essential. In fact, they were products designed to be ingeniously and uniquely profitable in search of a problem to solve.

This CFO was unimpressed by our proprietary products pitch, scoffing, "There's not an original idea on Wall Street."

Our guys finally stopped talking, the meeting was over, and we were packing up to leave. I asked the CFO, "What did you think? Was it a good meeting?"

"*Hell* yeah!" he said. "I got a lot done."

"What do you mean, you got a lot done?"

"Well, basically, I wasn't paying a bit of attention to whatever the hell it was those guys were talking about, so I went through my to-do list in my mind and ... well, I really got a lot done. Thanks for stoppin' by!" It was a long trip home.

In my first year at J.P. Morgan there was a wave of mergers that absorbed a slew of struggling rural hospitals in communities where the population bases were shrinking. My team and I arranged to pitch the CFO of one of those hospitals in Oklahoma, on the day before Christmas Eve.

We showed up in our tailored suits, Hermès ties, and Bruno Magli shoes. The CFO was one hundred percent oil-and-cattle country—tooled leather cowboy boots, leather fringe jacket, cowboy hat, huge glittering cowboy-themed belt buckle, and a gaudy pinky ring. Our dinner party looked like a sit-down between Tony Soprano and Colonel Sanders.

Getting him to talk deals and details at dinner turned into a conversational nightmare. Either he wasn't interested or none of it made sense, or both. We couldn't get his motor started. The only thing he seemed interested in was food. He had ordered barbecue and when his order came, his face lit up. "Boy, I sure do love these ribs." In fact, he loved anything pork, so that's all we talked about—sausages, ribs, tenderloin, pork rinds, bacon, scrapple, you name it.

It was like the scene in the film *Forrest Gump* when Forrest befriends Bubba, a black soldier, in Vietnam and they decide that after the war they're going to become shrimpers in the Gulf of Mexico. Bubba is obsessed with shrimp. "Shrimp is the fruit of the sea. You can barbecue it, boil it, broil it, bake it, sauté it. There's shrimp kabob, shrimp creole, shrimp gumbo, pan-fried .... "

Raised Catholic, I got along well with the Catholic hospital executives who occasionally made me feel like the altar boy I once was. A sprightly nun who was the finance chief at one of the large multistate health systems would greet me by grabbing a generous pinch of my cheek, as if to say, "I'm watching you, mister, so don't you try to pull any fast ones." I'd grown up with Kissing Tony so I felt right at home.

Goldman partners were encouraged to sit on boards of universities and hospital systems. It was tempting to pull strings to get to a reluctant CFO, but a bad idea as one of our teams discovered the hard way. Goldman had been trying to call on a particular CFO about a possible large financing for some time and had been getting the cold shoulder. The CFO wasn't answering his phone or returning calls.

Frustrated, one of the bankers went to a Goldman partner who had a major client who sat on the CFO's board to ask him to put in a good word with the CEO. That had the intended result—the CFO's assistant called and made an appointment. Our team was to fly from New York and Chicago to Phoenix to meet with him on the Friday before Memorial Day weekend, at nine o'clock sharp. That meant both of our guys had to fly in the night before, an inconvenience just before a three-day weekend.

The bankers showed up at the CFO's office on time and were ushered into a small, windowless waiting room. Nine o'clock became 9:30, then 10:00, then 11:00. The guys began to worry about catching their flights home for the long weekend. If they missed them, with all that traffic they might not be able to find a seat and be stuck in town a second night.

Lunchtime came and went. They missed their flights. Finally, at about three o'clock in the afternoon, the CFO came striding into the room wearing a sinister grin. "I just want you guys to know that I've decided to work with Merrill Lynch. In fact, we just finished one of the last meetings we'll need to put together a deal."

The bankers stared, slack-jawed, as the CFO continued, "Now, if you sons of bitches ever go over my head to my CEO or board again, I will personally see to it that you never get any work in this state. Enjoy your weekend, fellas!"

CHAPTER 7:
A PIT OF PYTHONS

Relentlessly curious, demanding, smart, intimidating, pragmatic, and hilarious. Those are some things investment bankers who've gotten to know him have said or thought about Lawrence Furnstahl, currently CFO of Oregon Health & Science University, a $2.5 billion public healthcare provider. I am one of those bankers.

Twenty years ago, when I first met him, he had a decade of experience under his belt as a financial executive in the not-for-profit hospital sector in Chicago. Our first encounter had seemed unfruitful at the time, but he would become one the most influential people in my career.

Furnstahl was interested in more than pork products, actually listened to our bankers when they came calling, and wasn't into head games or power trips. He was like a badger the way he dug and dug until he got to the bottom of a question. His quarry was always the right or best answer.

It's because of him that I first established myself as an independent financial advisor and sat on his side—the happier and more fulfilling side—of the table.

Furnstahl became the CFO of the University of Chicago Hospitals in 1987 before I transferred from Goldman's New York headquarters to its Chicago office. My new title was Vice President, Investment Banking, and my new role was covering healthcare and higher education clients in the Midwest.

Goldman in New York and Goldman in Chicago were two different animals. Being at the mothership provided ready access to the partners, trading desks, and technical experts, as well as camaraderie with more colleagues. Being in the heartland spared me from office intrigue, gossip, and getting sucked into the occasional crisis. I had much more freedom to pursue new business, which is what I enjoy most. Chicago was also a less stressful place to raise a family, which my wife and I had begun.

More of a marketer and new-business person by temperament, I liked being a larger fish in a smaller pond. The pace was slower, giving me more time to build lasting client relationships—my definition of long-term greedy.

Quite a few of us public finance lifers became so attached to our projects that, on rare occasion, we have visited the construction sites of important new buildings and written our names on a beam or some other part that will never be seen. The bankers, lawyers, accountants, CFO, treasurer, and others—anyone who worked on the transaction or planned the structure—assembled at the site to celebrate and memorialize the long and circuitous journey getting to that point and to express our hopes for the future. One of my signatures is hiding in the walls of Chicago's Northwestern Memorial Hospital. One day, when those buildings have reached the end of their usefulness, perhaps some eagle-eyed demolition workers will notice the signatures and ask, "Who were those people anyway, and what were they doing here?"

Furnstahl was one of my first calls in Chicago. Checking around, I learned he was a CFO with a reputation for being meticulous and a numbers guy—show me the data. He was also known as the whiz kid who financially rehabilitated one of Chicago's top academic medical centers. He had accomplished what experts much older than him, with decades of experience, had said was "utterly impossible." Consultants had recommended moving the hospital campus to an upscale suburb, an idea he and his board dismissed as ridiculous. Along the way he'd managed to ruffle quite a few feathers.

It started when he was a twenty-one-year-old budget analyst right out of college, working for his alma mater, the University of Chicago. The university owned a teaching hospital—University of Chicago Hospitals (UCH)—affiliated with its Pritzker School of Medicine. In the early 1980s, when the Medicare system for reimbursing hospitals began to tighten up, UCH was hemorrhaging cash and posting a lot of red ink—negative $23 million in 1984. It was encumbered by $90 million in debt with the prime interest rate hovering around 12 percent.

The new Medicare rules and the hospital's precarious financial health persuaded the university trustees that they needed to uncouple the school from the hospital. They decided to create a separate corporation. The university would still own the hospital but would not agree to guarantee its debt, hoping the restructuring would make UCH credit-worthy enough to refinance on its own merits. Either way, the hospital had to be rescued. It was highly rated by U.S. News & World Report and a large swath of Chicago's South-side residents depended on UCH, as did the Pritzker medical students and faculty.

A fresh management team was assembled, headed by Furnstahl's boss, who told him, "You're coming with me, Lawrence, and you're going to be a hospital administrator." Furnstahl was still a greenhorn. He knew a little bit about budgeting but nothing about healthcare or the banking business. He didn't yet know what he didn't know.

Before any refinancing attempt could begin, UCH needed a set of separate books. Its accounting system had always been integrated with the university's. A full scale audit and untangling was required. But senior bankers at the major New York investment banking firms who were invited to submit proposals turned their noses up. They declared it a hopeless mission to shape up UCH enough to be able to refinance its own debt. Some third party, a government guarantee, was needed but would have been a stretch to pull off.

"Not knowing that it was impossible," Furnstahl recalls, "I was given the job of investigating how it might be done. I connected with a bunch of young bankers at Morgan Stanley which, for some reason, allowed me to pursue the project and cobble it together. Had I known then what I know today, I would not have bothered to try. With their help we got it done."

Furnstahl earned the eternal enmity of those senior bankers and financial advisors who swore it was impossible. He made them look foolish and their firms flat-footed. He also annoyed Morgan Stanley's trading desk in New York the day the bonds were to be priced and sold. The process of setting bond prices—which would determine the hospital's debt service costs—was artfully mysterious (and still is). Across the board on Wall Street, public finance clients rarely understood it. They nearly always went along with whatever the trading desks told them. Not, however, Furnstahl.

"They started on the morning of the pricing on a conference call giving me a description of the interest-rate environment. The guys in New York on the other end of the conversation were going on about how the Israeli Air Force had just bombed Lebanon that morning.

"'Gee, that's a real shame.' I said. 'What's that have to do with our deal?'

"'Well, you see, the threat of war in the Middle East causes interest rates to spike. So that's gonna move the needle some from what we projected.'" A spike in interest rates would cause a corresponding drop in the price the bonds would fetch, leaving the hospital with less capital and more expensive capital than had been projected.

He was baffled. What was the connection between an incident in a never-ending conflict halfway around the globe and how much it was going to cost to get University of Chicago Hospitals back up on its feet?

"Wow!" he told the bankers. "Does the Israeli Air Force know they have this market power? Could they short our bonds, bomb Lebanon, and make some money?"

At that moment, I'm certain the folks on the speaker phone in the conference room at Morgan Stanley's New York offices were rolling their eyes at each other, making obscene gestures, and thinking, silently mouthing, or writing down the word "asshole," or something akin to it.

Furnstahl was thinking along the same lines. The deal was complicated enough as it was, and especially so for a newbie. The offering included various maturities ranging from one to thirty years. He just wanted to know his cost of capital. What he heard sounded like gibberish or double-talk, which is exactly what was intended.

The less clients know about the pricing process, the more flexibility the sales and trading desks have to finagle transactions in ways that boost the profit for the bank and its institutional clients who bought the bonds. When traders talk to clients about the price of the bonds, they talk about it going up or down in eighths, and when they talk about the interest rate, they talk about it moving up or down in basis points—0.0001 (1/100th of a percent).

The pricing process moves fast and the underwriters talk even faster, using terms that are bewildering to all but those who live inside the bubble: yields to call, yields to maturity, yields to worst, option and refunding-adjusted yields. They make obscure references and employ non-intuitive language. "Govvies are cheap relative to swaps," or "We've got an investor who wants to do a TOB with a higher coupon structure and the kick on the yield would be 50-75 versus par or deep discount." Huh?

Someone in Furnstahl's position, with his lack of experience, couldn't possibly absorb all that information in real time, couldn't calculate his cost, and sensed he was being played but didn't know how. His bankers were annoyed by his dumb jokes—"Could you say that in English?"— and his endless follow-up questions. Like parents whose young children keep asking "Why?" they probably wanted to strangle him.

When the dust had settled, Furnstahl, along with the Morgan desk, had achieved the impossible. UCH was able to refinance the $90 million of debt off the university's books onto the hospital's at a reasonable interest rate for the time. Furnstahl's education in the murky business of investment banking had begun.

Today, thirty years later, when he is in a similar situation, "I always say to the trading desk that I'm not expecting the Israeli Defense Force to be involved in this transaction. That inevitably leads to me telling them the story and they get the message—no BS. And now I always go to New York to be there in person so the people from the trading desk have to come and look me in the eye and explain what's going on, in English."

He says he was a little intimidated at first, but in time as he dealt with Wall Street, "It became clear to me that the interests of those well-dressed investment bankers who come down from the mountain in New York to talk to us lambs in Chicago were not aligned with ours. We were not, as I had been led to believe, all working together with the same goal."

Furnstahl was about a quarter century ahead of his time. For decades, public finance clients have treated their Wall Street bankers as trusted advisors and exclusive partners in raising the money to build airports, bridges, hospitals, and so on. A CFO who doesn't understand what he or she is being told will keep a tight lip for fear of looking stupid.

As incredible as it may seem, especially in the wake of

the 2008 Great Meltdown and ensuing Great Recession, most CFOs of public institutions have always thought their bankers were on their side. Part of the Goldman Sachs mythology was that being a client of the firm was a sign of legitimacy: "OUR investment bankers are Goldman Sachs! They take good care of us."

Not so much. It wasn't until passage of the Dodd-Frank Wall Street Reform and Consumer Protection Act in 2010 that investment banks were required to inform their clients in writing for each deal that, in fact, "the banker does not have a fiduciary duty to the client and does not operate in the client's best interest."

That such a disclosure letter should be required among professionals at that level sums up what's changed about Wall Street in the past thirty years. An institution that had been thought of as the guardian angel of growth and prosperity gambled away the rent money, had to be bailed out, and now must be kept on a short leash.

By the time I met Furnstahl, a few years after Morgan Stanley raised the $90 million he needed, he knew what he didn't know. Soon after I relocated to Chicago, he invited Goldman Sachs—my team and me—to meet with him about a round of refinancing. He was still using Morgan Stanley, so I was excited by the prospect of stealing some business from a competitor. UCH, I was sure, was about to become my first new piece of business.

Instead, he told me he wanted Goldman Sachs to be his financial advisor and just review a deal that Morgan Stanley was putting together as lead underwriter. For this service he was offering to pay us a fee of $15,000—less than what

Goldman spent each night on Town Cars.

Proud of securing my first new client there, but chagrined about the fee, I reported this to the Goldman mullahs in New York who greeted it with derisive laughter. "This is a joke, right? You're fucking with us for real, right? We're supposed to look over Morgan Stanley's shoulder and tell this guy how he's getting hosed? For $15,000 we're supposed to go piss off these guys we do deals with all the time? No way! Asshole!"

As ridiculous as the idea may have sounded, it was a foot in the door at University of Chicago, whose board of trustees included an alumnus who was a Goldman partner. The firm reluctantly went along with it.

The firm's queasiness underscores the collusive nature of the business. All the underwriting desks at the various investment banks partner on deals with each other all the time—a case of honor among thieves. Whichever firm is the lead bank running the deal book—in this case Morgan Stanley—sets the interest rate. The co-managers are expected to agree because that same day the roles will be reversed on other deals coming to market, sometimes only twenty minutes later for a different borrower on a different conference call. One underwriter doesn't piss off a competitor by publicly disputing what they're saying or exposing to clients the sketchy process of pricing.

Author Michael Lewis, in his book *The Big Short*, which tells the inside story of how Wall Street caused the 2008 crash, did a colorful job of summing up the state of things and the role of the big firms' fixed income trading desks. As stock prices plunged, panicky investors dumped them. In search of a "safe" harbor, they plowed the proceeds into bonds.

It was possible to get ripped off by the big Wall Street firms in the stock market, but you really had to work at it. Bond salesmen could say and do anything without fear that they'd be reported to some authority. Bond traders could exploit inside information without worrying that they would be caught. The only way to determine if the price some bond trader had given you was even close to fair was to call around and hope to find some other bond trader making a market in that particular obscure security.

The opacity and complexity of the bond market was, for big Wall Street firms, a huge advantage. The bond market customer lived in perpetual fear of what he didn't know. … [I]n the bond market it was still possible to make huge sums of money from the fear, and the ignorance, of customers. An investor who went from the stock market to the bond market was like a small, furry creature raised on an island without predators removed to a pit full of pythons.

Furnstahl was determined to avoid being one of those furry creatures and has seized many opportunities over the years to embarrass, call out, annoy, or otherwise make bankers squirm in their leather executive chairs. For example, every banker who calls on a CFO, treasurer, or debt manager with a deal proposal is obliged to bring a thick spiral-bound presentation book that includes a page of recently completed deals that are supposed to be comparable—comps. This information is included to help figure out how to estimate the most attractive price for the bonds so that the offering will sell out without being too over subscribed.

The bankers explain that there is a 50 percent chance the

rate will be higher and 50 percent it will be lower. The best estimate is supposed to be in the middle. It's a bit of a shell game because the comparables are chosen to fit a predetermined rate that the bank wants, not the other way around.

Furnstahl tells the banker, "Pick the comps that are better. I want to be on that end. Tell me the story behind them, why they're comparable, in English." As soon as he says that, the banker gets a little red-faced and stutters trying to explain why those aren't, in fact, true comparables.

Not only will bankers compare apples to oranges with a straight face, they'll go on to declare that their fruit experts have determined that the value of the orange is ten cents cheaper than the apple. Many public finance executives who lacked the expertise to understand the transactions they were doing, relying on inaccurate or misleading comparables, made decisions that will cost them and their institutions for decades.

On any banking team you'll find a junior analyst just out of college who the team is working twenty hours a day but who understands little of what's going on beyond what they can see on their computer monitors. When Furnstahl meets with a banking team and one of the senior bankers uses some jargon or inscrutable terminology, he will frequently turn to the junior analyst, who's supposed to just sit there patiently with his mouth shut, and say, "You know, whatever that was he just said ... I have no idea what that means. Do you have any idea what that means?" In Furnstahl's office, bankers are the furry creatures and he is the python.

Pricing in the municipal bond market, especially in healthcare, is a guessing game. The borrowing institution wants the investment bank to guess aggressively in its favor without being so aggressive that the deal fails. But the underwriting desks have no incentive to price aggressively. They are not primarily focused on the best interests of the investment banking client, a public institution with which they interact once every year or two when a financing comes up.

Underwriters are like air traffic controllers responsible for getting a steady stream of incoming jets—the deals— safely on the ground and the passengers—the bonds themselves—off the planes and on their way into customer portfolios. Their sales force is focused on their relationships with the big institutional investors who they want to sell the bonds to in order to earn the takedown—institutions they do business with every hour of every trading day. The higher the yield, the easier the bonds are to sell.

In his thirty-some years as an investment banking client, Furnstahl has seen most, if not all, of the things that can go wrong when it comes to the big day—pricing and sale. "Sometimes you don't get any orders for your bonds at all because you've priced the interest rate too low. Sometimes you get ten times the number of orders you want because it's too high and thus attractive to investors. At the end of the day, I want to get only exactly as many orders as I need."

The underwriting desk, however, wants the deal to be oversubscribed. At the end of *their* day, they want to avoid holding (owning) unsold bonds. Oversubscription gives them the flexibility to price the bonds to their best customers at what's still an attractive rate, knowing those customers will flip them the same day like shares in an initial public offering.

An oversubscribed deal also makes the underwriters look

good. These are people who tell their kids they're getting nothing for Christmas, and then on Christmas morning there are presents under the tree and everyone feels good. Nothing looks better for an underwriter than first telling the client their bonds will price cheaply (that is, at a higher interest rate) and then working the interest rate down on the day of pricing.

Not-for-profit institutions like hospitals, whose financial executives are not in the market every day, often don't know that there can be significant wiggle room in these transactions. The borrower who isn't paying attention often leaves a lot of capital on the table, capital that becomes the profit of the bank and its best customers. Furnstahl may be the CFO of a $2.5 billion healthcare system today, but he says, "I'll work hard to save a few bucks. You'd be surprised how much you can do with $200,000."

In 2009, with his encouragement, I swapped sides of the table and discovered the value and the pleasure of knowing exactly what the guys on the other side are thinking. It's more fun using that knowledge on behalf of the public institutions we all expect to be there when we need them, as opposed to working your butt off for some long-term-greedy cliché.

CHAPTER 8: REDHEADS AND BLUE COLLARS

"Eat what you kill," a familiar expression at the time, conjured an apt image—the largest and fiercest lions feasting on a freshly killed haunch of zebra while the lesser members of the pride watch from a distance, with the hyenas behind them, and the vultures beyond the hyenas. Many of us who worked in public finance, especially in the hospital field, were mere cubs compared to our trophy brethren in corporate finance.

When I started in investment banking, the team was more important than the individual. Gang tackling was rewarded. Piling on at the end was discouraged. There were star quarterbacks, running backs, linemen and receivers. Between then and the time I quit, the team model (everyone shares in the profits) was replaced with "eat what you kill": those individuals who brought in the client were paid better than the rest.

A dream of many public finance bankers is to move up the food chain into corporate finance. My decision to leave Goldman Sachs was in part because J.P. Morgan & Co. had folded its not-for-profit healthcare group into corporate finance and M&A. The fledging team I led was set up to close gaps in its coverage of hospitals and managed care companies.

It seemed like a good idea at the time but it turns out it's nearly impossible to retread a muni banker into a corporate investment banker. Not-for-profit and for-profit healthcare are fundamentally different businesses.

Not-for-profit hospitals are religiously, academically, or community affiliated. Until recently they operated exclusively within the US. Many have been in business a century or longer. They fund research and education; and their profits are reinvested in the communities they serve. For-profit hospitals operate for the purpose of maximizing returns for their executives and shareholders.

It was clear almost from the start that the not-for-profit healthcare group I headed didn't belong within corporate finance. At one of our first combined healthcare weekly meetings, the corporate bankers reported on the $60 billion merger between global drug giants Ciba-Geigy and Sandoz.

Then my team talked about the $30 million bond offering that Sister Michael Marie and Sister Veronica were planning for St. Mary's Medical Center in Indiana. The corporate folks didn't even try to feign interest or to conceal their derisive smirks. Our entire offering was less money than their fees. When my team was done, it was apparent to me that the merger with our corporate finance brethren was not going to work out. It was a source of humiliation.

Public finance clients are governmental entities or charitable corporations. They have large endowments of investable assets that need to be managed but no need for equity underwritings or dedicated experts in global corporate M&A. A city can't buy another the way Proctor & Gamble buys a competing maker of toothpaste or laundry detergent. Pennsylvania is not going to add the Massachusetts Turnpike to its toll-road portfolio.

To be in public finance you had to fight off those feelings of being small, corny, or insignificant compared to the corporate gladiators. As one young banker told the *New York Post* in 2014, "Everyone's always measuring their d – – ks. If I'm a Goldman banker, I go up to a McKinsey consultant and I'm like, 'My d – – k's bigger than yours.' "

Public finance isn't sexy, the plundering is limited, and public finance bankers aren't quite as obsessed with their anatomical dimensions.

Public finance banking was so far down the totem pole that in the 1980s it would have been easy for a couple of ambitious but corrupt investment bankers with a morally bankrupt lawyer and a crooked bond trustee to come up with a fictitious hospital in a fictitious town in a remote part of the country, cook up a fictitious board of trustees along with financial and other documents, float a $30 million insured bond deal, have the full amount wired into a Cayman Islands bank account, and be long gone by the time anyone noticed. The big Wall Street firms didn't bother doing any research on nickel-and-dime deals. It wasn't even worth getting out of bed.

One of the members of my "class"—those of us who came to Wall Street in the mid-1980s—who shared my worm's-eye view of the world was J. Patrick Sheehan, a public finance banker who became a good friend. He was with Wells Fargo in 2013 when he was tragically killed in an accident while a passenger in an airport limo on his way to meet and entertain clients.

Sheehan had an Irishman's jaunty but jaundiced wit. He once observed, "The annual report of a JPMorgan Chase, Bank of America, or Morgan Stanley is plastered with photos of a new computer chip laboratory in Malaysia, garment factories in Vietnam, cell phone factories in China, copper mines in Peru. That's international finance. That's where the transformational growth is. Municipal bonds? We're the redheaded stepchildren of investment banking."

People like Pat Sheehan truly love what we do, care about our clients, and find little to envy in the lives of our for-profit colleagues. For starters, the top corporate investment bankers—the ones author Michael Lewis once described as members of "a master race of dealmakers" and "a breed apart"—have always had to work like badgers to earn their cash piles. Those of us in public finance worked hard—sixty hours a week—but the people on the corporate side put in another twenty. Aside from work and sleep, they had at best a handful of hours a day, seven days a week, for their private lives. The corporate finance business is fickle, booming and busting just like the stock market, so those bankers are always on the lookout for a better job elsewhere.

Deregulation of energy, transportation, and banking unleashed five or so golden years of numerous and sometimes monster mergers during the early-to mid-1980s. Then came the so-called "program trading" crash in October 1987 that put an estimated 100,000 Wall Streeters out of work. The number of deals being done each year stagnated for more than half a decade. In Wall Street's bedroom communities across the harbor in Brooklyn, signs began to sprout that hadn't been seen in New York in nearly two decades (or since)—Apartment For Rent.

The next boom came in the second half of the 1990s when absurd valuations were attached to Internet IPOs that had no profits, a trickle of revenue at best, and hip names, like British e-tailer Boo.com, that have long since been forgotten. That boom peaked in 2000, just as AOL, a "new economy" dot-com, bought out Time Warner, a long-established media company that had three times the revenue and five times the number of employees. It was a $165 billion deal—one for the record books—that stuffed Godzilla-sized fees of nearly $100 million into the pockets of bankers at Morgan Stanley, Dean Witter & Company, and Salomon Smith Barney Inc.

The tech bubble began to deflate within months of the merger and then everything collapsed, followed by a deep recession. Many of the helpful bankers who had assured pension funds and other institutional investors that it was a fair valuation for the combined companies had been laid off or moved on by the time the scale of the disaster they helped create became clear. It is still, fifteen years later, widely considered the worst M&A deal in history and has become a permanent case study in business school curricula. In the end, the Time-Warner/AOL merger destroyed about $200 billion of value.

The for-profit side of the business can catapult a young banker into the one-percent class overnight. But to do that takes a killer instinct and the moral blinders to sell the "shitty" deals. Small wonder the casualty rate is high—according to some estimates nearly half of junior M&A bankers at leading firms quit within three years.

People in public finance aren't aiming to retire at thirty-five. In the past, they stayed in their jobs for decades, so it was hot gossip when someone in a senior position at a major institution quit to start a second career, retire abroad, or sail around the world.

Public finance clients always have financing needs, they never go out of business, and employment is usually steady. Unlike corporate M&A, you find few Ivy Leaguers in red suspenders doing business with Sister Michael Marie. Most people I have worked with over the years came from the public sector; had studied political science, economics, or government; and wanted to feel good about what they were doing.

Many of us also came from blue-collar or nontraditional backgrounds, like Lorraine McLaren, a thirty-four-year veteran of Goldman Sachs when she left in 2011. Lorraine could have been the prototype for the main character, Tess, played by Melanie Griffith, in the 1988 film *Working Girl*. It's the story of a young woman from a working-class Staten Island neighborhood who lands a job as a receptionist at a prestigious investment bank. Although she has no formal education or experience, she has ideas. Through a series of twists and turns, her business instincts and common sense propel her to the top of New York's financial circles.

Lorraine was about the same age as Tess when she started out in 1977. Like Tess, Lorraine was born and raised in a working class neighborhood of Staten Island. Her father was a union electrician. Like Tess, Lorraine went to work soon after graduating from high school but continued her studies at night school. And, like Tess, Lorraine felt out of place on the Street but loved the excitement of working in a zany, outrageous business.

By the time I left Goldman Sachs in 1997, Lorraine was deeply involved in the business side of projects, including the construction of major hospitals. She interacted with engineers and contractors whose work Goldman was assigned to review before payments were released. She was the only woman in the bunch and had to learn not to let her feathers get ruffled while supervising men who often treated her dismissively.

One of those projects was a new building that was part of New York Hospital in Manhattan (later merged with New York–Presbyterian, which is affiliated with Weill Cornell Medical College). Leading a tour through the construction site one day, one of the men in her group noticed a worker yelling her name over the clatter of equipment. It was her father. He happened to be working on a crew installing electrical equipment and was eager to brag about his daughter in front of his buddies: "That's my Lorraine, the big Wall Street cheese."

Lorraine had the unique experience of being on the front line during the dramatic transformation of Wall Street and especially Goldman Sachs. When she arrived in 1977, the firm was a small, intimate, familial partnership with a sterling reputation and just 1,500 employees.

When she left more than three decades later, Goldman was a public company employing 34,000, the largest full-service investment bank in the world, and one of the most controversial companies in America.

The firm had been stung by several messy scandals, including a scheme to manipulate commodities prices for essentials like aluminum, and for promoting those lousy mortgage-backed securities to clients while secretly betting against them. In the cataclysm that followed the 2008 crash, Goldman beggared a $10 billion too-big-to-fail loan from the US government. There were other black marks, but those were the principal ones that prompted journalist Matthew C. Taibbi, writing in *Rolling Stone*, to describe Goldman as "a great vampire squid wrapped around the face of humanity, relentlessly jamming its blood funnel into anything that smells like money."

The *New York Times* dubbed Goldman's traders the "Bandits of Broadway." A Goldman trader named Greg Smith, who resigned in the wake of the financial crisis, wrote an op-ed and then a book about the "morally bankrupt" people he worked with who referred to their clients as "muppets." Even the *Wall Street Journal* weighed in, so outraged by the government bailout it rechristened the firm "Goldie Mae."

When Lorraine first went to work for Goldman, the partners were typically people whose elder relatives had been partners and had come up through the ranks. That changed in the 1980s when the firm started hiring MBAs from brand-name schools.

As the MBA crowd moved up and into senior positions, they went back to their alma maters to recruit the next generations, young men and women who were easily dazzled and seduced by conspicuous consumption and prestige.

Unlike previous generations, they felt no obligation to honor a family legacy. They showed up for their new jobs with a sense of entitlement conferred by their pedigrees.

In spite of the knowledge, skill, and competence she achieved over the years, Lorraine, like myself, never quite shook the outsider feeling. When we first started working together, we quickly discovered we had a similar point of view. We did our jobs without thinking about much other than the vague faith that if we worked hard the rewards would follow. We shared blue-collar backgrounds and were both bemused and sometimes horrified by the excess.

"I had no ambition to become fabulously rich," Lorraine says today. "I was making more money than I'd ever dreamed I would, so it was easy to focus on providing value and being altruistic. That sort of thinking didn't exist anywhere else at the firm, and those of us in public finance were for the most part willfully naïve. We lived in our own little world."

CHAPTER 9:
DON'T TOUCH THAT DIAL!

Gusts of arctic wind howled through the canyons of Wall Street, stinging and numbing my face as I sprinted the three blocks between the job I'd quit moments earlier at Goldman Sachs and my new employer, J.P. Morgan & Co. As in, actually running—in a suit, tie, dress shoes, and my long wool coat, unbuttoned in my haste, flapping in the wind. I was lugging a briefcase bulging with papers and personal items. Not the most dignified way to make a career change. It was January 1997.

The distance between 85 Broad Street, then Goldman's home office, and 23 Wall Street, famous as the one-time home of J.P. Morgan, is just over three football fields—350 yards. On a busy weekday it can be walked with purpose in about five minutes. On that day, however, seconds counted.

Muttering "Sorry!" and "'Scuse me!" as I bobbed and weaved through clutches of pedestrians, I fought my way to the storied intersection of Broad and Wall Streets. On one side a grand statue of George Washington stands in front of Federal Hall, the site of America's first capitol building, where he first took office and also where the Bill of Rights was first ratified. Washington's gaze is directed toward the heart of capitalism and the symbolic financial center of the universe—the New York Stock Exchange. In his line of vision is also the entrance to the original and fabled House of Morgan.

I needed my new ID badge and then to get to a phone as fast as I could. I mentally flipped through my address book, triaging the calls I'd have to make in the next few hours. Clients, some of them longtime friends, needed to be reassured that the switch I was making was good for everyone, that there was no scandal lurking in the shadows, and that their capital structure and planning remained healthy, secure, and on track—with me, no matter where I was.

I knew that by the time I had stepped into the Goldman elevator after giving notice, my former colleagues had divided up my list of accounts and gone to their battle stations. They would be calling up my clients to reassure them that the switch was good for everyone, that there was no scandal lurking in the shadows, and that their financing plans remained sound and secure—right where they were, at Goldman. The battle for my book of business—a Wall Street ritual whenever a banker or broker jumps ship—was underway.

This warlike process of defection and deception has ended at US banks now that they have adopted the British human resource policy of "garden leave." The employment contract that most new bankers have to sign today provides for a forced vacation once they give notice. It may be several months, longer for senior bankers. They remain on the payroll during that period but are sent home and barred from entering the office, prohibited from communicating about work with anyone at the bank, and cannot work for any competitor. The joke is that all they are allowed to do is weed their gardens.

When I started at Goldman I had been an idealistic, wide-eyed twenty-something out to save the world while conquering a piece of it. Ten years later, both Goldman and I had changed and the time was right for me to move on. I knew some people would ask themselves and each other, Who the hell leaves Mount Olympus voluntarily? What's up with Mark?

The story behind the story was that the new head of public finance had decided to close most of the regional offices, including Chicago, and move the bankers back to New York. About a half-dozen of us made the very personal decision to stay in Chicago where our families had become established. In January, after a Christmas Party themed "The Last Supper," after our bonuses had been paid, we all quit.

At that point, my most important clients included some who had been with me from the beginning, nearly a decade earlier. I was certain many would follow me to J.P. Morgan. Others would need stroking. Either way, I wanted them to hear the news from me first.

When I finally got inside J.P. Morgan's investment banking offices at 60 Wall Street. I set myself up in a small conference room that had been prepared for me, complete with a prerecorded message on my voicemail. Once settled in my new command headquarters, I began dialing.

"Hey, it's Mark! Guess what? I've decided to leave Goldman and join J.P. Morgan and I couldn't be more excited."

It was just like the scene in the film *Jerry Maguire* when the character played by Tom Cruise, a professional sports agent who has just been fired, spends frantic hours on the phone begging his clients, one after another, to come with him to his new agency. Meanwhile, the people at his old agency are trying to get them on the phone first, to convince them to stay.

To my clients I said, "I've left Goldman and I'm now at J.P. Morgan, but I'm still your guy and here's why it's going to be so much better for you."

My former colleagues at Goldman were telling them, "Hey, guess what? Crazy thing. Mark left. No, absolutely not. He wasn't fired. I don't know the details but listen, we just wanted to let you know we really, really love you and we have another great team to work with you, so stay right where you are. Don't touch that dial!"

I'd never switched horses before and didn't realize until recently what a major disruption it is for the clients. They have to take time from what they need to be doing and meet with a succession of teams of unfamiliar, grinning bankers, all competing for business that is perceived as up for grabs.

The experience taught me that the clients did not belong to me, even though it felt that way. At the end of the day, the CFO of a health system tells the board of trustees, "Goldman Sachs recommends ...," not, "Mark Melio recommends ...."

Although bankers want to believe that their clients are true-blue friends who will all come running after them to a new firm, only about a third of a typical banker's clients will follow him or her. Another third will stay with its existing firm, and a third will use the change as an opportunity to shop for a new one.

There were good reasons for me to leave Goldman when I did. J.P. Morgan was an up-and-comer in the municipal bond market. Goldman's long-term-greedy mantra had grown stale and sounded increasingly hollow as the firm pushed hard to cut costs and make as much money as fast as it could in advance of going public. Record profits in the quarters leading up to the initial public offering would fatten the premium on the price of its initial share sale.

The partner system was ending, so that was no longer an incentive to stay. The firm's two hundred or so partners had become preoccupied with their anticipated windfalls, which, by some estimates, would eventually make each of them richer by an average of $75 million.

Under those circumstances I was wary of the firm's continuing commitment to a redheaded stepchild like public finance, which contributed a pittance to profit compared with the rest of its operations. I was also worried that Goldman would pull out of pubic finance altogether to avoid headline risk—an unforseen scandal.

The federal government had been on a crusade to clamp down on political bribes, kickbacks, collusion, and influence peddling in the award of municipal bond underwritings. Municipal finance has always been a political swamp and any county executive or public authority director will tell you that, at least in the early days, he who contributed the most to the dominant party got the business. Pay to play had been the unspoken standard practice. Bankers routinely wrote checks to the campaigns of politicians they hoped to do business with.

Now the Feds were exposing a few examples of corruption to send a message to the market. The month before I gave notice at Goldman, one of the most powerful people in the business, Mark S. Ferber of Lazard Freres, had been sentenced to nearly three years in jail for his role in a secret kickback scheme between Lazard and Merrill Lynch. It was a shocker to those on the inside of the business. Sleepy public finance had suddenly become radioactive. I worried that Goldman might decide the downside wasn't worth it anymore. A number of firms had already exited the business that year: Credit Suisse First Boston, Lazard, Donaldson Lufkin & Jenrette (DLJ), and Chemical Bank.

The history of my new employer, J.P. Morgan, was the flip side of Goldman's Jewish pushcart-peddler origins. The seed money for J.P. Morgan, named for its founder J. Pierpont Morgan, had been provided by Morgan's wealthy father, a banker who had inherited his grubstake from his wealthy father, whose ancestors had emigrated from Wales in 1636. The firm had been founded before the Civil War, when Pierpont Morgan was a broker for railroad stocks, a particularly corrupt corner of Wall Street in those days.

When the War Between the States began, Morgan paid $300 (about $10,000 in 2016 dollars) for a substitute to take his place in the Union Army, a common practice among the wealthy. According to historians, one of Morgan's first big scores was buying five thousand rifles for $3.50 each from an army arsenal and flipping them to a Union general in the field for $22 each. The rifles turned out to be defective—soldiers who tried firing them got their thumbs blown off. A congressional committee discreetly investigated the deal, but a federal judge let Morgan off the hook with a ruling that the financier had merely fulfilled a valid contract and therefore was not liable.

Morgan would later acquire U.S. Steel and monopolize the steel industry and then do the same in the railroad business. By 1900, Morgan's holding company controlled 100,000 miles of railroad, half the country's mileage. His firm bought up much of the Atlantic steamship capacity to control the market for the millions of people fleeing Europe to immigrate to America—the same route my ancestors took. During World War I, the firm won a monopoly on financing the war effort for England and France.

Commenting on some of Morgan's activities, Louis Brandeis, who would later become a US Supreme Court justice, once wrote that the firm and its partners "control the people through the people's own money." You might say some things never change, or at least not that much.

The robber baron era ended with the Crash of 1929 and the ensuing legislation prohibited firms like Morgan from using depositor money to underwrite securities and other investments. The Glass–Steagall Act of 1933 forced the Morgans of the world to choose whether theirs would be a commercial bank (think checking accounts, lending, and corporate treasury services) or an investment bank that could invest and speculate but only with the money of its partners and investors.

J.P. Morgan chose to operate as a commercial bank because investment banking was held in lower esteem. In

1935, Morgan spun off its investment banking business to two Morgan partners, grandson Henry Morgan and Harold Stanley, who founded Morgan Stanley.

My fears about Goldman's commitment to public finance would prove to be unfounded, but my move was right anyway. J.P. Morgan was in a better position and their municipal bond department was in a better growth cycle. I became the head of a group and then later head of all the firm's public finance activities.

Most importantly, I could work out of the Chicago office and thus not disturb my family. The transition was smooth and the future looked bright.

CHAPTER 10:
DYSFUNCTION JUNCTION

As my old firm, Goldman Sachs, was preparing to go public, my new firm was about to go through an equally dramatic transformation.

A year and a half after my arrival, Wall Street was hit with one of those periodic crises that seem to threaten our entire financial system. A huge hedge fund, Long-Term Capital Management, that did business all over Wall Street and paid an estimated $100 million a year in transaction fees, went short-term bust. J.P. Morgan's stock, which had been rising, sank along with the rest of the financial industry and the inevitable flurry of consolidations began as stronger banks vultured the weak.

Mergers in the financial industry accelerated after passage of the 1999 Financial Services Modernization Act, which undid the Glass–Steagall rule against mingling commercial and investment banking. When a glowing profile of J.P. Morgan appeared in *Fortune* magazine, I sensed that an effort was being made to gussy up the firm for sale, and that is exactly what happened in 2000. We were sold to another venerable brand name—Chase Manhattan Bank—and the surviving firm became JPMorgan Chase.

The new company combined a huge, aggressive, but Balkanized consumer and commercial bank with a smaller, cozier investment bank with a storied history, now managed by a new generation of scrappy, ambitious executives. The gears began grinding from the start.

The commercial bank had very different relationships with its clients and offered multiple service lines. On the other side, those of us in investment banking had no interest in selling our clients on lockboxes, credit cards, and other bread-and-butter services.

We covered the same client base but from different perspectives. On a gut level, the clash was over who owned the client relationship—turf conflict. Investment banking and commercial banking mistrusted each other. Furthermore, Chase Manhattan brought with it the legacy cultures of other banks it was in the process of merging with over the years, including Chemical Bank, Manufacturers Hanover, and Texas Commerce.

Within the combined JPMorgan Chase, there were now multiple fiefdoms. In my area we were referred to as "heritage J.P. Morgan." In 2003, JPMorgan Chase acquired Chicago-based Bank One, a commercial bank that had become a behemoth by buying up its competition throughout the Midwest. By mid-2004, all of Bank One had been absorbed. Now there were people who were considered "heritage First

Chicago," "heritage Bank One," "heritage Chase," "heritage Chemical," "heritage Manufacturers Hanover," and so on.

Turf scrimmages escalated into all-out conflict. The ignorant and condescending investment bankers, myself included, scoffed at the commercial bankers. "Those lockboxes and PCards you have with your customers, or the checking accounts you have with them, are fine and nice, but we make a couple of million per deal in underwriting, swap, and credit fees. When it gets to the bottom line, by comparison you're irrelevant in the relationship." (I later learned I couldn't have been more wrong.)

The commercial bankers argued that their products and services provided an annuity revenue stream in the form of annual fees. "It may only be a million-dollar annual relationship, but it's a million dollars every single year, and that number goes up as they add more products, services, and complexity."

I was an investment banking loyalist and believed that we were the true rainmakers. It seemed obvious—commercial banking is a commodity activity, like digging coal out of the ground a chunk at a time. My self-important view of investment banking was more akin to medicine—we were trusted specialists, experts who offered sober, impartial advice and skillful execution of large, essential, big-picture transactions whereas the commercial bankers were primary care physicians.

In time, I began to understand that the commercial banking relationship, unlike investment banking, is rarely interrupted or taken away. At most our transaction profits reached $2 million and we would have to fight for it every time the client came to market.

It was more complicated than just that. The investment bankers called on the CFO and Treasurer. They made presentations to and interacted with the CEO and the board of trustees. The commercial bankers called on the cash manager, or assistant treasurers and vice presidents in charge of billing, accounts receivable, and accounts payable.

Commercial bankers were not financial analysts who were trained to drill down and come up with a concrete plan to structure a particular client's bond offerings. Investment bankers had no interest in selling commercial banking's pencils and paperclips, but in the spirit of promoting the new JPMorgan Chase, I began assigning representatives from the commercial side to join us for important client meetings. What I learned was humbling.

Aimee Trepiccione was a product partner for the commercial bankers. Her portfolio included health insurance companies, hospitals, and health systems and her role was to market what we dismissed as the paperclips—revenue-cycle services—to clients on both sides of the banking aisle. She began joining our investment banking teams' client dinners with CFOs and Treasurers.

I was surprised to discover that they were eager to hear what she had to offer and to seek her advice. We, on the other hand, had to wait our turn to talk about what we thought was the important stuff.

It was a reminder that important stuff can't happen if a borrower does a poor job of managing its cash flow. Nevertheless, there was grumbling from investment bankers who were miffed about having to compete for "their" client's attention.

Although she was caught in the middle, Aimee was astute and together we did our best to find ways to make it work. "In our internal meetings, we tried to find a way to bridge the gap," she recalls. "Our group was called 'specialized industries' because we focused on healthcare and higher education. In meetings between the investment and commercial bankers we went through the client list name by name, trying to determine which side had the strongest relationship, how we could cross-sell investment banking, and vice versa."

We invited Aimee to speak to our healthcare investment banking group meetings at JPMorgan Chase and I spoke at the Chase healthcare group's meetings. It was a challenge to find common ground and sometimes I got frustrated and more than a little annoyed at the lack of talent on the commercial banking side, and even their manners. Their people would sit through the investment banking presentations looking bored and chewing gum.

One day I decided I'd had enough. I stood up in one of the Chase meetings and laid it on the line.

"Do you want me to stand here and tell you I'll ask my bankers to introduce you to our most important relationships and connect you with the CFO? Sure. In fact, I promise you that I'm going to tell my people to do that.

"Is it going to happen? Probably not. Why should my bankers introduce you to their clients? We have no use for your credit. We have our own credit facilities and we have our own book of business.

"If you want to sell them treasury services or whatever, God bless. Good luck with that. We'll be as helpful as we can, but the powers that be base our revenue solely on investment banking services. Besides, when the commercial bank gets involved with our clients it multiplies the opportunities for important things to get screwed up, like a glitch with a client's payroll that wouldn't be our fault but would put our people on defense and at a disadvantage."

Today, as a financial advisor to clients, I've learned that it's important for the relationship manager (typically on the commercial banking side) to be there for the routine day-to-day needs as well as the underwriting milestones. Back then, commercial banking looked like a messy ball of string. Today it all makes sense, so long as the investment and commercial bankers can actually work together toward a common goal.

Another transformation within public finance subsequent to JPMorgan Chase acquiring Bank One was the change in leadership within the municipal bond department. A hedge fund manager and former currency trader was brought in by Jamie Dimon to run the entire department in 2006. This ousted the former head of public finance, who had grown up in the business and assuredly led us for more than a decade while fostering teamwork and growth.

I was promoted to co-head public finance with a wise, seasoned, politically and governmentally focused former Bank One manager. We were constantly challenged and second-guessed by our new manager, who was oriented to the trading desk. Our department even had a new glitzy name and acronym—TECM—which stood for Tax-Exempt Capital Markets.

Our new boss knew nothing about municipal finance

but he was so smart and confident, he didn't care. He walked around for a month with a notepad and pencil and interviewed virtually everyone in the department, as well as anyone at JPMorgan Chase who had any connection to municipal bonds—the commercial bank, wealth management, derivatives, and U.S. Treasury trading.

At the end of the month, in one of our senior management meetings, he announced that he had figured it all out. He proceeded to show us a cartoon-like drawing of some type of complex plumbing contraption. He explained that issuers' and borrowers' financing needs got fed into the top, like in a meat grinder. Those bond deals then worked their way through the pipes—derivatives, trading, underwriting, and syndication—and out the end came the money for JPMorgan Chase to pay our bonuses.

I'd heard similar "plumbing and pipe" concepts from other former traders who had been annointed as heads of municipal bond departments. Soon enough, the traders were calling the shots within public finance, stepping into this dysfunctional breech with the commercial bank and the results were disastrous.

They took control of the investment bank's credit products without any sensitivity to the essential nature of the public service and not-for-profit sector entities. They felt no connection or loyalty to the public finance client base, no respect for long-standing relationships, and ran roughshod over financing arrangements and protocols that had taken years to develop.

Then the traders tightened the screws, jacking up pricing and stifling the amount of credit the investment bank would extend. The traders had a scarce and valuable resource and took full advantage of it just as clients needed credit the most—to get through a brief but agonizingly difficult period. This tactic was consistent with the firm's focus on battening down the hatches but it was felt far and wide as "clients be damned."

The DNA for that attitude was as old as the firm and most eloquently articulated in 1901 by J. Pierpont Morgan himself. Challenged by a reporter about his manipulation of the price of railroad stocks, he is quoted as saying, "I owe the public nothing."

We were being told, "That's it. No more extending credit. We do underwriting business, investment banking, sales, and trading." That's when my job became much more difficult. When I tried to make the case that we needed to extend credit to a long-term client hospital or health system, as we always had in the past, the answer was, "Absolutely not." I had prided myself on being the guy who clients could count on to try to find a way to get to yes. Now there was none. It was all about "no."

When we asked why, the traders said, "We think a lot of healthcare credits are going to go bankrupt."

"Wait ... WHAT?!"

To those of us who had spent years in public finance, and working with hospitals in particular, this was an absurd argument. Hospitals rarely go bankrupt, and even if it looked like a particular hospital was in trouble, no politician in his right mind would let it happen without making a public-spirited to-do. A county, city, or state government would step in to keep the facilities open and solvent, or a merger would be arranged with a stronger entity.

The traders didn't have a clue and made it clear that credit would only be extended to our clients in rare circumstances. Even if we did, it would have to be expensive enough that the investment bank would be guaranteed a huge profit to compensate for the supposed but nonexistent additional risk. In some of my conversations with the traders, they had the gall to suggest that bankers and clients needed a lesson in developing appropriate capital structures, as if the clients were too dependent on bank credit.

This shift put us in a difficult position with clients. Suddenly, the commercial bankers became Johnny-on-the-spot. They could say to our clients, "Hey, guess what? We've got a lot of credit. And we're not nearly as baffling as the traders who are now running the investment bank."

In our internal meetings, we discovered that even if the investment bank had arranged a credit portfolio for a significant client, the commercial bankers would come in and offer the same basic deal at totally different prices. It was the same JPMorgan Chase credit facility, but it was being offered and priced differently by two different parts of the bank.

It seems unlikely that CEO Jamie Dimon was unaware of this bizarre internal competition. It is equally unlikely that heads of each department would have risked telling him. It was a problem they should have been able to resolve on their own and neither would have wanted to take a chance that in the process of getting it settled by Dimon they could wind up with the short end of the stick.

The commercial bankers wanted to go out and sit with

"our" CFOs and be able to say, "You want credit? We have credit. It might be kind of expensive, but the investment bank is not going to give it to you. And by the way, because you need our credit and we have it, we're also going to put into our credit agreements that you have to give us a certain amount of other business to offset the extension of our balance sheet."

The message in the marketplace was tough but clients couldn't go anywhere else and hear a different message. Any firm with both investment and commercial divisions was dealing with the same problem. Ironically, my old employer, Goldman Sachs, was one of those that didn't have that problem because they were still just an investment bank.

Wall Street was changing and changing fast. Financial engineering, derivatives, proprietary trading, and ever-riskier bets were replacing old-fashioned relationship banking. Long-term greedy was long since dead and buried. Leverage and short-term profit were where the action was.

The traders must have thought the bankers were playing solitaire on their computers all day, or traveling around the country going to fancy restaurants and ordering expensive wine. The bankers considered the traders Neanderthals and knew that they, the bankers, were the ones who brought the clients into the firm, and that they, the bankers, were the ones representing the investment bank to the issuer clients.

Even today, traders will tell you, "We're the ones who are making the money." Bankers will reply, "Touchdowns look easy from the end zone. We're the ones who got the ball down the field."

J. Patrick Sheehan, my former J.P. Morgan colleague and

friend who worked in public finance at Wells Fargo before his death in 2013, experienced the same friction. He once told me, "The bosses look at us as inefficient overhead, loss leaders. They see eighty bankers taking up office space and bringing in less revenue than five people on the trading desk. The traders seem to resent that the flow on the trading desk comes from the deals, the new bond issues we bring to market. Otherwise, the traders would have to make their money with what's out there on the secondary market, the same business everyone else is fighting over.

"It's similar to the car business. A new car dealer doesn't just sell a new car to a buyer. There's a used car trade-in to make money on, service, insurance and warranty contracts to sell, and repeat business from brand loyalty. A used car dealer has to bid against everyone else for product and there's no other source of revenue."

Sheehan also drew a parallel with Las Vegas, an appropriate comparison considering the business we were in.

"Vegas makes its money on gambling, but to lure people you have to have good, clean, cheap entertainment for Mom, Grandma, and the kids—Celine Dion, Penn & Teller, Cirque du Soleil. That's us. We bankers are the wholesome floor show. Meanwhile, just down the hall Dad and Grandpa are gambling away the kids' college funds."

Although the business had changed a lot since I started, a couple of bright spots for me, at least, were that I had risen through the ranks to a senior position at JPMorgan Chase— head of public finance. On the lighter side, my promotion to managing director brought along with it an "impressed by celebrity status once removed" moment. Every serious candidate for managing director at J.P. Morgan had a "sponsor," someone the candidate did not know. I later learned that mine was Jamie Grant, who was based in London, and was the older brother of the actor, Hugh Grant.

Two months after my promotion to head of public finance, in March 2008, Bear Stearns, an eighty-five-year-old investment bank known for its aggressive tactics and which, a year earlier, had been named the "Most Admired" securities firm by *Fortune* magazine, imploded. The US Treasury Department and Federal Reserve facilitated the sale of its remaining assets and liabilities to JPMorgan Chase for a fraction of its former valuation.

My new boss had come up through the ranks of the trading desks and earned a reputation as a trading genius and guru. Now he headed the firm's trading operations. That I was now reporting to him was a clear sign of the withered influence of investment banking in general and public finance in particular.

The first time I met him, he wasted no time confirming his bias. He walked into my office, pointed a finger at me, and said, "Mark, I just want you to know I hate bankers."

Stunned into silence, a wave of heat rose up the back of my neck. I'm so screwed, I thought. I'm the senior-most investment banker in public finance. Everyone I manage is a banker. My new boss is telling me he hates bankers. I'm SO screwed!

He must have seen the look of horror on my face because he quickly added, "Look, I don't know you but I've heard good things about you and our working relationship is going to be terrific. But I still hate bankers."

That was a seminal moment in my career, the beginning

of the end of my tenure in investment banking. But before that would happen, it fell on my shoulders to help clean up the wreckage of Bear Stearns. For the rest of the year I would spend a good chunk of my time "Up In The Air," George Clooney–style, closing offices and laying off bankers, including some long-time colleagues who were also friends.

CHAPTER 11:
SWAPPED OUT

Between 1987, when I first arrived at Goldman Sachs, and 1997, when I sprinted over to J.P. Morgan, Wall Street morphed from the plodding caterpillar it had been for half a century into the dazzling butterfly that was the tech boom. By the late 1990s the economy was humming and the air was filled with the scent of easy money.

My career had started during a stock market crisis along with a massive financial scandal that killed off the savings and loan segment of the banking industry. So much had changed since then, in the economy and on Wall Street.

When I first joined Goldman Sachs, financial news was to most Americans just white noise. The principal and dominant outlet was the staid, grey, and reliable *Wall Street Journal*. Other than the periodic scandal highlighting crooked dealing or wretched excess, Wall Street news was of interest mainly to those who worked in, or depended on, the financial industry.

During my decade at Goldman, interest rates began what would turn out to be a long, choppy decline from levels that today sound like a borrower's nightmare and an investor's fantasy. At the peak, a plain vanilla one-year bank CD paid as much as 12 percent. In my corner of the world, public finance, the decline and occasional volatility along the way was good for business. It was an easy sell when state and local governments and public institutions like hospitals could cut their cost of capital by periodic refinancings. We investment bankers had more business to chase and the Wall Street pythons that author Michael Lewis wrote about had more furry little creatures to devour.

Most of the people Lewis refers to—the ones I know, anyway—are personable, caring, and well-intentioned. But as a German proverb warns, "Look before you leap, for snakes among sweet flowers do creep." What feels reptilian about Wall Street is the way the firms seduce their people, who in turn seduce their clients into believing the bank will deliver the absolute lowest cost of capital while omitting mention of costs like the so-called distribution cost of flipping.

As fixed income returns retreated, retirees, wealthy individuals, and the portfolio managers at pension and mutual funds began moving into equities. Prices rose, buying begat buying, CNBC was born, and the Internet boom was on. The man in the street suddenly knew what an IPO was and the hot new way to make money was to quit your dull corporate job and become a day trader. Everybody could be a genius because to lose money in equities you had to work at it—the S&P 500 was seven times higher in 1999 than it had been twelve years earlier, when I joined Goldman Sachs.

Like real butterflies, which live for a few days or at most a week or two, the good times died in 2000. The day traders went back to their day jobs, and three years after it peaked, the S&P 500 Index had shed half its value. That year, 2003, Bernstein Research (Sanford C. Bernstein & Co.), a leading Wall Street think tank, issued a report on the financial industry that began, "The institutional equities business is in trouble."

The Bernstein analysis failed to take into account the resilience and physics of Wall Street. Like a balloon, squeeze one end and the other gets bigger. Take away one source of income and Wall Street will find another to replace it. The solution was financially engineered investment products—derivatives. Smart young "quants," computer-savvy quantitative analysts (think grads of Carnegie Mellon, MIT, and University of Chicago), were applying game theory to trading strategies, designing computer programs, creating algorithms, building high-speed transaction networks, and structuring derivatives. Derivatives were supposed to lower the net cost of capital for borrowers able to take some risk and hedge against interest rate swings and credit defaults.

The point of all this history is to show how Wall Street as an institution came to think and behave. The business had come a long way from the days when it was thought of—in theory, anyway—as the engine of national prosperity, the Mecca of capital formation, overseen by partnerships of prudent men who jealously guarded their good names.

Whoever said it first hit the nail on the head—by the 1990s Wall Street bankers had become people who help you with problems you wouldn't have had without them. The Street had become an engine of wealth creation for itself.

The smartest people in the room had been busy thinking up problems or identifying risks for which they could invent complicated, profitable financial products—like derivatives—to solve.

This trend got a huge boost in April 2002 when Federal Reserve Chairman Alan Greenspan—Mr. Prudent himself—gave a speech in which he said, "New financial products have enabled risk to be dispersed more effectively to those willing, and presumably able, to bear it. Shocks to the overall economic system are accordingly less likely to create cascading credit failure."

Six years later, in the middle of the economic meltdown he helped set the stage for, Greenspan expressed "shocked disbelief" at the "self-interest of lending institutions." That ranks right up there with British Prime Minister Neville Chamberlain's "peace in our time" treaty with Germany, signed a year before Hitler invaded Poland.

Greenspan had been Fed chairman for two decades, a man living and working inside a bubble. Before that he had come of age in the era of the old Wall Street—the one with partners and principles. His glowing endorsement in 2002 of derivatives gave the new Wall Street the green light, the keys to the vault, a license to steal. And that's exactly what happened. Hundreds of trillions of dollars of derivatives were created and sold, blowing an astronomical bubble of theoretical value.

Meanwhile, firms like JPMorgan Chase, Citi, Merrill, Morgan Stanley, and Goldman Sachs wasted no time exploiting the opportunities. Goldman in particular had figured out a way to legally trade on inside information with no risk by using what it knew about the aggregate trading behavior of its big institutional clients against those same clients. It was the same principle behind selling those "shitty" CDOs to customers while simultaneously shorting them.

Author and Wall Street critic Michael Lewis, writing in *Vanity Fair* in 2013, called it a war of robots.

> The robots were absurdly fast: they could execute tens of thousands of stock-market transactions in the time it took a human trader to blink his eye. The games they played were often complicated, but one aspect of them was simple and clear: the faster the robot, the more likely it was to make money at the expense of the relative sloth of others.

Everybody had robots—computerized trading programs. The robots of institutional customers—pension and mutual funds—were programmed to send out buy and sell signals based on a complex set of predetermined circumstances. If the shares of McDonald's rose above a certain price or by a certain percentage, to use a vastly oversimplified example, the computer might tell a portfolio manager to buy shares of Burger King.

Wall Street had robots, too, and firms like Goldman had figured out how to program their computers to predict what their institutional customers were going to do, before they did it. Bernstein Research's 2003 report explained it thus:

> Much of the simple execution business will evolve to automated algorithm-based trading systems (known in the trade as "traders in a box") that can compete with alternative trading systems. ... We expect proprietary

trading to increase within the "winning" brokerage firms. The consolidation of client demand through the securities firms will provide insight into market demand. ... We expect [Wall Street firms] to make use of this demand information to profit from more aggressive proprietary trading ... *As proprietary trading becomes more important to profitability, current customers of the major brokers will find themselves evolving from client to counterparty.* [Emphasis mine.]

Counterparty, in this instance, is just a polite word for prey. According to Bernstein, the big Wall Street firms, the predators, could effectively frontrun their customers—turning their clients into counterparties—without breaking any laws. According to a footnote buried deep in the report:

This is not "front running." Trading in front of client orders is not acceptable behavior in the equity market, but using aggregate demand data captured from execution activity to trade other securities is acceptable.

The Bernstein researchers had apparently done their homework. In an exchange of letters between Goldman's Washington law firm and the Securities and Exchange Commission, the company asked for and received an opinion letter blessing the concept of proprietary trading—gambling with the firm's own capital while simultaneously handling client transactions.

Goldman was already making a fortune on proprietary trading by the time the Bernstein report came out. The first year Goldman got the SEC go-ahead, 1999, the firm's revenue from trading and "principal investments" tripled over the previous year. In 2000, when many firms were hurting and JPMorgan Chase reported a 20 percent decline in earnings per share, Goldman Sachs posted a record year and a 12 percent increase in earnings per share.

In my little corner of this ecosystem, the financially engineered product we sold our public finance customers was the interest rate swap. Swaps first emerged in the UK in 1981 as a tactic to hedge interest rates. A borrower such as a hospital system might swap its variable rate debt—which is exposed to market and other risks— for debt with a fixed interest rate. The borrower's goal is to lock in a lower fixed rate than could be achieved by issuing conventional fixed rate bonds through an investment bank.

Like fuel, corn, oil, or currency futures, swaps are derivatives—they have no actual value in and of themselves. The terminology used to describe interest rate swaps tells you all you need to know.

The size of the swap is the "notional" amount. The goal of the swap is to create "synthetic" fixed or variable rate debt. Swaps have mark-to-market valuations. There are basis swaps, cost of funds swaps, LIBOR basket swaps, forward starting swaps, tax language swaps, and total return swaps, just to name a few. There are also options on swaps, called swaptions. Boiled down, these transactions are basically exchanges of cash flows.

If that sounds kind of sketchy, you're in good company. The same year that Alan Greenspan gave derivatives his blessing, Warren Buffett dismissed them as "financial weapons of mass destruction." The 2008 catastrophe proved Buffett right many times over.

Selling swaps to my clients involved some number crunching and plenty of guesswork. We would compare the histories of fixed- and variable-rate debt. We would look at how many times over the previous thirty years tax-exempt interest rates were above or below the current levels. We would run the numbers to make a case for swapping variable to fixed or vice versa. Then we would try to convince our clients that they were better off letting our firm negotiate the deal—just trust us—rather than putting it out for competitive bidding to multiple banks.

That was the meat on the bones of what became the swap business—using our relationships with clients to get them to negotiate trades with us, which was fundamentally imprudent but made the firm a ton of money. That was my job, to make money for JPMorgan Chase.

We bankers convinced ourselves that our analysis and expertise justified the millions we made. Worst-case scenarios were inconceivable and it didn't matter that clients barely understood how swaps could work against them. As bankers we were compensated and patted on the back when we made a lot of money for the firm. There was no reward for saving a client from screwing itself.

Had I drunk too much of the Kool-Aid? Like the people I worked with at the time, I believed we were giving clients the firm's best advice. What was good enough for Greenspan should be good enough for our clients. We were lulled into the "notional" idea that these complex financial products— ignoring the risks—would save clients a lot of money while making a lot of money for the bank.

The head of a major financial advisory firm at the time

once told me that auction-rate securities swapped to a fixed rate were a no-brainer. He had never worked on Wall Street, was oblivious to the fuzzy development cycle for these new products and he knew nothing of the failed auctions that sometimes resulted. Yet he and his team were advising clients to structure as much of their debt this way as they could—in the billions.

Beyond ignorance, financial advisors with derivative advisory practices had a strong profit motive to encourage clients to enter into swap contracts. Some even recommended their clients swap more than their outstanding debt—orphan swaps. This reckless practice is akin to gambling.

When we couldn't persuade a client to let us privately negotiate a swap and they chose to put it out for bid, behind the bankers' backs the competing trading desks sometimes colluded. From recorded phone calls and emails it later came out that our traders would call their counterparts at another bank and say, "On this XYC Health System swap, why don't you lay low and then when ABC Airport comes next week, it'll be our turn to lay low?"

The swap business grew into a monstrous, opaque, black-box money machine. The reckoning came in 2008 as flaws in those derivatives became apparent. In public finance, the interest rate swap reckoning for JPMorgan Chase took the form of a sordid scandal—the insolvency and eventual bankruptcy of Jefferson County, Alabama.

Jefferson County was under a Federal Environmental Protection Agency consent decree requiring an extensive upgrade to the local sewer system. County officials sold bonds to finance the project, using a banker with

Raymond James & Associates, a small broker-dealer based in Florida. By November 2002, that banker had been hired by JPMorgan Chase, bringing with him $3 billion worth of Jefferson County sewer bond business. It included more than $2 billion in auction-rate bonds and interest rate swaps. It was all adjustable-rate debt, all privately negotiated, and obscenely profitable.

When the pythons got done with Jefferson County, JPMorgan Chase—along with Bear Stearns and Bank of America—had loaded the county up with $5.8 billion in interest rate swaps, the most of any county in the country and, according to press reports, pocketed fees of $120 million. Along the way, bribes totalling $8 million had been paid to local brokers who in turn bribed at least one public official. It was a rat-breeding contest.

In 2008, when the bottom dropped out of everything and rates went the wrong way, the county ended up insolvent with an additional $275 million of debt. Jefferson County filed for bankruptcy in 2011 with debts of more than $3 billion, making it the biggest municipal bankruptcy in US history. JPMorgan Chase's head of municipal derivative sales was fired, barely escaped criminal prosecution, and the civil suits brought against him and others arising out of the catastrophe were still unwinding five years later.

In the end, the Jefferson fiasco cost JPMorgan Chase a fine of $75 million and forfeiture of $650 million in future fees the firm claimed it was owed. Although I had nothing to do with it, this mess landed in my lap in February 2008, soon after I was promoted to head up JPMorgan Chase's tax-exempt banking group. My job was to help the "workout group" clean it up and also deal with the Bear Stearns takeover.

That's when my new boss marched into my office, announced that I was now the new head of public finance, and said, "Just so you know, I hate bankers!"

CHAPTER 12: SLAUGHTER ON MADISON AVENUE

The year I became head of public finance at JPMorgan Chase was another historic turning point in Wall Street culture. In the same way that 1929 was a defining moment for earlier generations, the year 2008 will be a defining moment for those millions whose retirements were cut short or delayed, who lost their homes and businesses, or who found themselves jobless.

As luck would have it, my 2008 started with a promotion, a challenge, and a front-row seat to a drama that had the entire country holding its breath, pondering the unimaginable—a wholesale write-down of assets that could lead to Great Depression II. My vantage point also happened to be from the box seats of a winning team. Chairman and CEO Jamie Dimon would later be dubbed "the last man standing" for having navigated JPMorgan Chase through the storm. *Newsweek* magazine reported a year later that, "Jamie Dimon was the only chief of a major bank to have properly prepared for the hundred-year storm that hit Wall Street. Starting the year before, his firm had been aggressively dialing back its exposure to mortgages—particularly of the subprime sort—while others were sitting tight."

It's human nature to find irony and coincidence in major events after the fact, and 2008 is a mother lode. A week or so after New Year's, Bear Stearns sponsored an international professional squash tournament. A glass room was erected inside Grand Central Station's Vanderbilt Hall and for a week commuters crowded around to watch. It was gaudy, fun, and irreverent, traits that reflected the popular image and culture of Bear Stearns—the boys from Brooklyn who, according to legend, started out poor and worked hard to get rich, as legally as possible.

James E. "Jimmy" Cayne, the firm's longtime chairman and CEO, had gotten his start in business in Chicago as a scrap metal salesman and cab driver. He once said his youthful ambition was to be a bookie. More than four decades later, the firm he'd led for twenty years had a reputation for being able to keep valuable secrets. Their trading desk did a lot of the business for wealthy individuals, hedge funds, and other fast-money clients who wanted to avoid drawing attention to their moves. When Bear Stearns traders started loading up on or selling off a particular stock, the market sat up and took notice. Insider trading suspicions had swirled around the company for years.

So Bear Stearns was more of a handball sort of place, whereas squash was upper crusty, having gotten its start in 1830 at Harrow, an exclusive British boarding school. Today it is played in formal courts at clubs, not against the brick wall of a nearby garage. Just sixty days after that tournament, a pubic relations gimmick to burnish the firm's image, squash is what Wall Street did to Bear Stearns's stock price when JPMorgan Chase absorbed the company for pennies on the dollar—and even then only with Federal Reserve loan guarantees.

The death of Bear Stearns was a long time in the making—a year of bad news and a steadily declining share price. The damage accelerated in March 2008 when the bottom began dropping out of the derivatives market. Cayne was forced out. The Treasury and the Fed were desperate to save Bear from outright bankruptcy. There was a well-founded fear that its default would have a domino effect and bring down the whole system.

The firm had loaded up on mortgage-backed securities and then leveraged its bets like an all-in poker player. At one point the firm had on its books "notional contract" amounts—numbers on paper—of more than $13 trillion in derivatives. When the dust had settled, those contracts were essentially worthless.

That Bear Stearns, a seventy-seven-year-old company that had survived the Crash of 1929 and the Great Depression, could be in such deep trouble had been unthinkable to many right up to the end. Just five days before the news broke, a viewer of CNBC's *Mad Money* asked the bombastic host, Jim Cramer, if he should be worried enough to take his money out of Bear Stearns. Cramer shouted into the camera, "No! No! No! Bear Stearns is not in trouble."

The news that Bear Stearns was being vultured broke on a gray, windy Sunday, March 16. I knew it was coming because it was my job, but there had been a steady stream of articles and commentary for months that hinted the firm's future was uncertain. Now there was no future and I would have to deliver terrible news to many people who'd been making a great living working for a company that had a good reputation and a scrappy culture.

Nearly 15,000 people worked for Bear Stearns at the time. Fortunately, I only had to be the bad news bearer for about 150 people who wouldn't survive the merger. The news was especially devastating because other firms had just gone through massive layoffs and there were no openings to be found.

I flew in from Chicago that Sunday and spent most of that day on the phone, answering questions, giving instructions, connecting dots, and planning the next few days. Our group—Tax Exempt Capital Markets—caucused at 6:30 Monday morning and then we walked across the street to the Bear Stearns offices—the shortest walk I'll never forget.

The sky had cleared overnight and the early spring sun poured down on St. Patrick's Day in New York, home of the largest parade in the world. It starts at 47th Street on Fifth Avenue. The marchers—bands, politicians, and a wild assortment of drunks in leprechaun costumes—were forming on Vanderbilt Avenue, a parallel street we had to cross to get from our offices at JPMorgan Chase to the glittering forty-seven-floor Bear Stearns building.

Unlike some branded skyscrapers, Bear Stearns had theirs built to order rather than renaming or rehabbing an existing building. That was the ultimate status symbol of arrival—Bear had become a top-tier Wall Street investment bank and it was going to be around for a long time.

The building occupies an entire block and was designed for one tenant. On a square base, the octagonal tower soars to a crown-like glass design at the top that gives it the feel of an English castle.

The firm had moved in just six years earlier. No expense was spared in tricking out the Bear Stearns offices. A huge circular meeting room with a massive donut-shaped table that seated forty could have accommodated the UN Security Council and then some in both size and appointments.

Now 383 Madison Avenue, the pride of Bear Stearns, was about to become the property of JPMorgan Chase and, according to some insiders, the only Bear asset that was actually worth anything. You could write everything else down to zero, it was said, and the acquisition of Bear was still a good deal just to get that building. For JPMorgan Chase it was a lucky break. The firm was preparing to spend $2 billion to move across the Hudson to New Jersey. Instead, JPMorgan Chase's name is over the door of a premier Manhattan address it got, relatively speaking, for a song.

As soon as we stepped out of the elevator into the main trading desk area you could feel the hush of anxiety and despair. The firm's stock had traded as high as $93 a share three months earlier but JPMorgan Chase was paying only $2 a share to pick up the shattered pieces (later raised to $10 a share).

Bear had encouraged employees to invest their retirement funds and take their bonuses in the firm's stock. By 2008, employees owned nearly a third of the shares and many of them, on paper, had become wealthier than they'd ever dreamed.

The look on many faces that morning reflected the

obvious—a lot of people had lost everything, including their jobs. There was anger, fear, bewilderment, and a lot of questions about what was going to happen next.

It made perfect sense for JPMorgan Chase to acquire Bear Stearns, although until that point Jamie Dimon had shied away from acquiring another investment bank. Six months later, when Morgan Stanley looked like it was going to go the way of Bear Stearns, then-Treasury Secretary Henry Paulson offered Dimon the chance to pick up Morgan Stanley in a similar deal—essentially for free. Dimon is said to have pointed out that an investment bank needs about 10,000 bankers around the globe. That's how many JPMorgan Chase had. So did Morgan Stanley. While reunifying the House of Morgan had sentimental appeal to some, putting the two firms together would result in a bloodbath.

The takeover of Bear Stearns was just that and JPMorgan Chase, having brokered hundreds of mergers, knew the drill—identify the best talent that comes out of the combination and follow the merger math, which would ordinarily be $1 + 1 = 1$. In the case of Bear, since we were in the midst of such a bad market environment, the headcount merger math was to be $1 + 1 = 0.75$. For every 100 JPMorgan Chase bankers and 100 Bear Stearns bankers, only 75 in total would remain and 125 would no longer have a job. By the time it was done, the number was closer to 135 people, many of whom had survived the annual culling of JPMorgan Chase's bottom 10 percent. What I had to work with was muscle.

Beginning St. Patrick's Day 2008, I sat in a small conference room across from Bear Stearns's municipal bond trading floor for what felt like months and one by one began the process of interviewing everyone in the banking group at Bear Stearns trying to identify and retain the best. I couldn't delegate those decisions because all of the JPMorgan Chase bankers under me were part of the math. They were just as worried as the Bear Stearns folks.

The experience made watching the movie *Up in the Air*, released a year and a-half later, difficult, especially the scenes where the main characters were delivering the fatal blows. I had to tell a lot of people, including some of my JPMorgan Chase colleagues, the same sorts of things that the character played by George Clooney did in the film, although not nearly as elegantly. "Your position is no longer available," and, "It's important not to focus on the 'why' but rather spend your energy thinking about your future."

The decisions about who would stay and who would have to go were based on profitability and performance. I knew JPMorgan Chase's numbers and I had a list of Bear Stearns clients and deals and some idea of revenues earned for the prior year. Through multiple conversations and behind the scenes fact-checking, I had to figure out who generated what revenue, and what their level of contribution was to Bear Stearns—whether they were a finder who brought in new clients, a minder who focused on keeping clients, or a grinder (worker bee). Or, were they the piling-on sort—a follower rather than a leader?

Of all the banking types, finders are the most valuable. Finders bring in the new business. Good minders can turn it into annuity revenue. Grinders keep the trains running on time but good minders are checking up to make sure they do.

The person who'd never make the cut is the poor schmuck

who is assigned to a house account, works hard, but does not bring in any new revenue or, worse, loses the account. That gets you an automatic firing squad.

Wall Street being a place that pays out the biggest rewards to the most aggressive, there were political crosscurrents to deal with, such as, "Hey, you aren't keeping my buddy? We've worked together for five years and now you want to break up a winning team?" One banker with connections managed to get a state governor to call Jamie Dimon on his behalf. Another leaned on a state treasurer to lobby for him.

The reactions of bankers who were let go or whose jobs were "no longer available" ran the gamut. Some were so blindsided they just shook their heads in stunned silence. Some were enraged. Fists were banged on desktops and doors were slammed.

Those I felt worst about were the people who, at the end of the conversation, stood up, politely shook my hand, and said, "I'm sorry it's not going to work out for me." I could handle incredulity and anger. But I still get a knot in my stomach when I remember those who said, "I wish you the best of luck. Thanks for a great run."

My own position was also being evaluated, although my promotion at the end of 2007 had been reported in the business press, a visible vote of confidence. The execs who had been running Bear Stearns's public finance department had more years under their belts but they had a lot of baggage. The culture of Brooklyn scrappiness had apparently included some sordid, Brooklyn-style seaminess.

Just three months earlier, two Bear Stearns bankers in Texas pleaded guilty to bribing public officials to win municipal bond deals. A Bear Stearns banker in Chicago had been indicted in a larger public corruption investigation involving a hospital project and would end up pleading guilty.

A Bear Stearns banker in Florida who'd brought in more than a half-billion dollars in underwriting business from a county where his wife happened to be a commissioner spent eight months in jail on fraud-related charges.

In the context of the bank's collapse, the Bear Stearns brand was wearing out. Meanwhile, JPMorgan Chase had gotten its own black eye for its role in the historic bankruptcy of Jefferson County, Alabama. Academics and journalists had begun looking into the huge growth in municipal underwritings that preceded the 2007–2008 credit crisis and discovering what goes on where municipal finance and politics intersect—bribery, influence peddling, illegal campaign contributions, collusion, favoritism, and so on.

Looking back on it now, I believe I was made head of public finance at JPMorgan Chase because the not-for-profit hospital and university sectors are less political and thus less prone to shady practices. Hospital administrators and university finance chiefs don't have to stand for election so they are focused on more important stuff, like growth, integration, and the bottom line.

A county commissioner who takes a bribe to steer a municipal bond deal to a campaign contributor is unlikely to be an experienced health system CFO type with a sharp pencil behind his ear making the tough decisions. Bankers in the not-for-profit sectors where I live tend to personally reflect the cultures of their religious or academic institutions. While we are all hired guns, we're more like missionaries than mercenaries.

The downsizing that followed the Bear Stearns takeover took several months to complete and was as educational as it was stressful. I had to sit with people from our legal, compliance, and HR departments to explain the strategy and make the objective business case for picking each person to let go and minimize the bank's exposure to discrimination claims.

This complex puzzle sometimes resulted in keeping people that didn't make sense to the outside world. We had to lay off good people and when we did their colleagues would sometimes come storming into my office outraged that we were keeping others who they thought were less productive.

When I allowed myself a few moments to reflect, the experience was surreal, unlike any situation I could ever have imagined. Most of the time I focused on the big picture, which was exhilarating and challenging—to end up with a stronger JPMorgan Chase with a best-of-class team of bankers.

It was a heady, center-of-the-universe moment in time and I never forgot what my boss had said to me when we first met: "I hate bankers." The goal was to have a fortress balance sheet to withstand the economic hurricane. The bankers were all about getting to yes for their clients. We were the good cops. To the traders, our clients were just counterparties and beyond that mostly pains in the ass. The traders loved being the bad cops. They were all about getting to "no." And now they were in charge.

One way or the other, I knew the end would eventually come for me as well.

CHAPTER 13:
THE HYPOCRISY OATH

Until my last couple of years in investment banking, I got a lot of personal satisfaction serving public and charitable institutions in medicine and academia—noble enterprises established for the public good.

My clients referred to Goldman, JPMorgan Chase, and the banking teams as "our" trusted advisor, much as they might introduce someone on their staff as "our" chief of neurosurgery. Like the doctors who worked in their hospitals, who take the Hippocratic Oath to put their patients' interests above all else, our clients trusted us to do the same thing for them.

When I look back now, knowing how Wall Street took advantage of municipal bond issuers in particular and torpedoed our economy in general, I'm chagrined to realize that the trusted advisor I saw in the mirror each morning was illusory. I genuinely cared about, liked, and was committed to serving my clients, but the firm's rule was more of a Hypocrisy Oath: Love thy client, but first, put JPMorgan

Chase's profit ahead of all else.

When previously unthinkable cracks started to appear in the credit markets in 2007, my beliefs and sense of fair play hadn't changed from twenty years earlier when I first arrived at Goldman Sachs. Wall Street, on the other hand, was not the place I thought it was in 1987. The collusive, predatory practices we know about now were just becoming apparent, like dead fish at low tide. I had worked within the system for two decades but I shared with my clients a sense of betrayal.

In the early days of my career, when a public finance bond deal was oversubscribed, we bankers—innocently, unknowingly, and unwittingly—would high-five each other: "Look how many investors were dying to buy these bonds!" We assured our clients that this was a sign of how creditworthy and how attractive to investors they were, and how brilliant and persuasive we were. It never occurred to us that demand was high because the bonds had been underpriced to produce a highly attractive yield.

What was I thinking?

When a new bond issue was sold, I had always assumed that the familiar brand-name mutual fund companies bought those bonds to hold to maturity for their conservative, tax-exempt funds. When I found myself on the other side of the table, I discovered that the trading desks first sold them to their regular and best customers—including professional day traders—who flipped them within hours for a quick buck like stock IPOs.

Thus the Mom and Pop retail investors who ultimately ended up owning those bonds and/or our borrower clients paid a hidden tax—the spread. It was an inside job, an undocumented kickback of sorts by the sales and trading desks to the customers whose high-frequency activity generated a lot of the firm's trading revenue.

These deals used to take place in the regulatory shadows where nobody would notice. The fast-money crowd may have been perfectly within their legal rights to flip what they bought, but we—the investment banks—were not giving clients the service and efficiency they were promised. Our clients' cost of capital could and should have been lower, as we assured them it would be. But the practice was well obscured. Complaints were rare and those that did come up were not pursued or taken seriously. We were untrustworthy advisors.

One particular swap transaction while I was at JPMorgan Chase illustrates how banks make money on their clients' confusion. The deal involved a hospital system in the West which had a trustee on its board who was lobbying the CFO to do a floating-to-fixed rate swap. The goal was to lock in the absolute lowest capital cost to fund a major expansion. The trustee's day job was CEO of a savings and loan company and thus was perceived by the other directors to be an expert. They did not understand that he had no experience in public finance and that he was a bit of a risk-taker.

Following the "expert" board member's direction, the hospital system CFO told us he would execute the swap with us on a negotiated basis, which is in essence a no-bid, no-competition contract. Negotiated swaps are more costly but allow public borrowers to choose which bank or other institution will be the counterparty. They help less credit-worthy borrowers get access to capital, but at a higher cost.

In this case, the customer had good credit. A true trusted advisor who put a client's interest first would have argued against a negotiated swap for the obvious reason—the bidding process tends to lower the cost of capital. But we at JPMorgan Chase just stood back, folded our arms, and kept our mouths shut, knowing the profit on the deal would be larger the way the board member wanted it done.

As we went through the process, our swap trading desk estimated that JPMorgan Chase would make about $500,000 to $1 million on a transaction of about $100 million or so. That seemed high compared to other deals I had been involved with, but not so high as to be outrageous. A couple of hours after the bonds had been sold, the swap desk called to tell me our profit was around $4 million. I was stunned. It was good news—so good I had a spasm of Catholic shame.

What does an investment banker like myself, afflicted with a conscience, do with the knowledge that our swap desk had picked the customer's pocket for an extra $3 million? We couldn't tell the hospital that they screwed themselves, or that we made a ridiculous amout of profit. Hear no evil, see no evil, speak no evil.

The folks at JPMorgan Chase saw this windfall as confirmation of their good judgment in having promoted me to head of healthcare, but I had no basis for patting myself on the back. Nevertheless, in theory I would receive a bigger year-end bonus because it would be calculated on an estimate of how much profit we made for the firm. It made no difference whether it was by bringing in new business or because of some trading desk hocus pocus.

What could have happened? Among a number of possible

explanations, one of the simplest is that the market rallied and the desk kept the benefit instead of passing it on to the client. Another is that the swap desk snuck or stuck in much more liberal "tax language" which increased the likelihood that the swap would either be terminated by JPMorgan Chase or would trigger a much higher interest expense for the hospital.

Had I understood at the time what was behind it all I could not have buried my head in the sand the way I did. The details came out later and so did clues to character. The swap trader moved on to another firm where he committed other infractions that got him sent to jail. Ultimately, the swap was restructured at a significant loss to the bank.

This behavior, however—exploiting confusion or ignorance—is the norm on Wall Street and it hasn't changed much.

In December 2015, RBC Capital Markets, the investment banking arm of Royal Bank of Canada, mishandled the sale of an ambulance company and short-changed investors by rushing into a buyout by a private equity firm RBC was courting for other business. It was a blatant conflict of interest, like Coke's investment bank using its client's corporate secrets to get Pepsi's business.

A Delaware Supreme Court ruling found that RBC was also trying to double-dip by earning an additional fee for providing financing to the buyer of the ambulance company. In other words, RBC was going to get paid by the seller and the buyer, another clear conflict. The Delaware court— considered the most authoritative word on most business law in the US—said that RBC had purposefully created an "information vacuum" for its client.

RBC was ordered to pay $76 million in damages. The story's author, mergers and acquisitions lawyer Ron Barusch, wrote, "It all makes RBC sound pretty bad. But the truth is that many of the things RBC did aren't so different from what investment banks across Wall Street do every day. And let's be clear: investment banks are riddled with conflicts."

There are many examples over the years of banks winking or looking the other way in order to enable the sale of bonds for dubious projects dreamed up by ambitious public officials, their business pals, and local celebrities. Municipal bonds have been used to build failed golf courses and civic centers that were touted as "enhancing the quality of life," and to support business developments that crash and burn.

One of the outliers in this category ended in March 2016, with federal fraud charges being filed against Wells Fargo Securities for its role in underwriting a $75 million municipal bond deal. The main purpose was to fund a startup video game company that had agreed to move its offices from Massachusetts across the border to Rhode Island.

The Securities and Exchange Commission said the bank, in league with the bond issuer—the Rhode Island Economic Development Corporation—failed to disclose the true financial picture of the startup. The chairman and majority shareholder of the game developer, 38 Studios, was the former Red Sox pitching ace Curt Schilling—an unfortunate last name to have under the circumstances.

"By lending money to a private company owned by a local sports hero," *The New York Times* reported, "state officials had hoped to stimulate jobs and lure other businesses to relocate to Rhode Island, which had been hit particularly hard by the recession."

According to the SEC, Wells Fargo cut a side deal with 38 Studios, which agreed to pay the bank an additional $400,000 if the bond sale closed. Wells Fargo was going to collect a toll from both parties. The secret side deal was never revealed to investors, nor was the fact that the company's executives knew beforehand that the net cash raised would not be enough to keep the company afloat.

When the dust had settled, the taxpayers were out the $75 million plus an estimated $20–$30 million more in related expenses; the net assets of 38 Studios added up to a negative $130 million; and Schilling was out his original $50 million investment. All told, nearly $300 million in value would end up being written down to zero.

Court cases that came out of a wide-ranging SEC investigation into bond trading practices revealed that traders in mortgage-backed securities had been lying about the prices of bonds they were selling. That's almost impossible to do in the stock market, but in the bond market it's not only easy to do but hard to detect.

A *Wall Street Journal* story about one of those cases reported, "The markets for certain types of bonds have long lacked clear prices, making it hard for investors to determine whether they are getting a fair price as they buy and sell. Brokers make money by buying bonds for less than they sell them; the difference is known on Wall Street as a spread. A broker can artificially widen that spread by exploiting the ignorance of the investors on both sides of the trade."

Just like those bundles of overrated mortgages that

imploded, in public finance there were deals that were initially offered on a "priced to sell" basis. A good example were Build America Bonds, taxable municipal bonds that carried special tax credits and federal subsidies for either the bond issuer or the bondholder. They were created as part of the American Recovery and Reinvestment Act of 2009 with the intent of reducing the borrowing costs of state and local governments with so-called shovel-ready infrastructure projects.

Some underwriting desks initially had no idea where they should be priced. They just didn't want them on their balance sheets and priced them to fly off the shelves.

One of the deals that was dropped in my lap to supervise after the fact was the financing of a wine museum in Napa, California. The project was the brainchild of Robert Mondavi, considered the George Washington of the Napa wine industry. His wife persuaded him to buy and donate an empty lot as the building site. It was next to a tire store in Napa, a charmless little farm town. The real wine country was not in the town of Napa, it was outside of town along the main highway, Route 29. Aside from the museum, it was a town of coffee shops, grocery stores, farm supply and equipment retailers, and other services for the many agricultural workers who live there.

The museum was named Copia, for the Roman goddess of wealth and plenty (as in cornucopia, the horn of plenty). Mondavi kicked in $20 million in seed money to design and build an 80,000-square-foot facility. When it was done, there were two exhibition galleries, two theaters, classrooms, a demonstration kitchen, a Julia Child–themed restaurant, herb gardens, and reflecting pools.

The rest of the cost of Copia was financed by donations and municipal bonds that were issued by the local redevelopment authority and which carried a good rating from bond insurers like ACA Financial. The key to success in the financial business is shoving as much of your risk as you can onto someone else's plate. In this case it was ACA Financial, one of several self-described monoline insurers (one product only) that sold insurance policies against bond defaults. ACA had been quietly and serenely insuring bonds for some thirty years.

The price of the insurance depended on the credit rating and stability of the borrower, among other factors. Bond insurance premiums on hospitals, for example, were on the high end because hospitals, unlike city governments, in extreme circumstances can just close the doors and go out of business. A good credit rating and bond insurance helped keep down the cost of raising capital.

Bond insurance had become so common, and defaults so rare, that the expense was considered more of a nuisance fee than a major cost. In a case like the Copia financing, the borrower—the museum (via the local redevelopment authority)—buys the insurance and pays the premium. The policy guarantees to make investors whole if the issuer defaults. As a result, the bonds earn a higher rating.

The Copia project was ambitious and the creditworthiness of the bonds was predicated in part on the museum promoters' prediction that the world was going to beat a path to its door. Copia was such a slam dunk to become the mecca of American foodies, the crucible of innovative American cuisine, that it presumptively called itself "The

American Center for Wine, Food & the Arts."

The museum raised nearly $50 million from private donors, mostly Mondavi, and the rest by issuing about $70 million in insured municipal bonds. The result was an impressive, swanky, modern yet classical edifice and grounds, with a staff of high-priced experts and a full-time operational crew and administration.

The museum's grand opening, planned long in advance, happened to fall on November 18, 2001—two months after the September 11 terrorist attacks on the World Trade Center and Pentagon. Ground Zero was still smouldering. We had boots on the ground in Afghanistan looking for Bin Laden. The public wasn't in the mood for food, wine, art, and especially travel, which had lost much of its allure in this scary new world.

Copia limped along for six years, losing millions—as much as $12.7 million in one year alone. Investors who were paying attention may have been concerned, but the bonds were insured. In some investors' confused minds, that was a guarantee almost as good as the FDIC insurance on bank deposits.

"We never had anything to worry us about the safety of ratings back then," remembers Anne S. Morse, an expert in healthcare finance. For seven years, including the worst of the financial crisis, she was an executive with Ambac Assurance where she specialized in healthcare and retirement living.

Like others who choose public finance, Anne's journey started off in a different direction, a dream to become a physician. Then she discovered she had an advanced case of hemophobia—fear of blood. Inspired by her father, a successful entrepreneur who started from scratch in the brokerage business, she channeled her interest into the study and practice of hospital financial management.

Ambac had been around for more than thirty years when she went to work there, after a stint in the fixed income division at Lehman Brothers. Ambac had been the incubator and creator of municipal bond insurance. The company was founded in 1971 when Ambac first began to sell it. Four years later, the business got a boost and gained legitimacy when the unthinkable almost happened in New York City—debt default.

By 2005, Ambac was one of a group of companies competing for a basket of business—underwriting and insuring mortgage-backed bonds. Business was also good for tax-exempt debt. As interest rates floated down, issuers were in the market more frequently with refinancings.

"In the public finance arena, the bond insurers had always had AAA ratings from all the major rating agencies—Moody's, S&P, Fitch," Anne recalls. It was a given that if it was good enough for the rating agencies, it was good enough for Mom and Pop. Insured tax-exempt money-market bond funds with rock-solid brand names—Franklin, Vanguard, Fidelity, for example—grew and flourished on the strength of unassailable AAA ratings.

The idea that a public institution like a hospital system might default on its debt was laughable. It still is, but much like what later happened to me at JPMorgan Chase as the markets and the banks got tough, Anne watched helplessly as public finance got punished for what was killing the subprime mortgage market, and the economy. Due to failed auctions, yields on otherwise AAA insured, tax-exempt debt spiked as high as 12 percent around the same time that the

Fed funds rate was peaking at 5 percent.

The housing bubble finally topped out in 2006 and by 2007 home prices had begun to recede. As it turned out, the bond insurer, ACA, had insured a dung pile of high-yield subprime mortgage bonds that were beginning to look shaky as default rates began to rise. *The Big Short* is the story of what happens when everyone who could buy a house, and plenty who shouldn't have been able to, bought at least one. Many were financed based on so-called liar's or no-doc mortgage applications on which anybody could claim whatever income they wanted and no one bothered to check if it was legit.

Millions of people who had equity in their homes had been persuaded that it made financial sense to mortgage them to the hilt during the run-up in values. They spent the money on additions (Hey, it increases the property's value!), vacation homes (Hey, we'll rent it out and it'll pay for itself!), boats and other goodies (Hey, you only live once!). When housing prices sputtered and started to fall, homeowners found themselves under water, upside down, owing more than their houses were worth. As the recession deepened, those who found themselves out of work were unable to keep up the mortgage payments and went bankrupt or just walked away, sometimes leaving the keys in the mailbox for the bank's repossession crew. The dominoes began to fall.

Rating agencies downgraded billions in mortgage-backed securities and by the end of 2007 ACA Financial had foundered in a sea of guarantees it couldn't honor. Copia somehow made it through 2007. The man behind it all, Robert Mondavi, died in May 2008, spared by six months the indignity of seeing his dream go bankrupt and his pet project closed and padlocked.

What happened to Copia was happening on a massive scale across the country. Billions in public-private partnerships to build and maintain toll roads, schools, public golf courses, and civic centers had been financed with revenue bonds whose credit ratings crumbled when the recession hit and tax revenues fell. All of the bond insurers were wiped out in a short period of time. It was fierce and sudden. Treasuries and municipals were where people like Bill Gates and Warren Buffett had stashed their most essential cash hordes. Now a mountain of those safe, insured municipal bonds were suddenly unsaleable.

The brokers at places like Goldman Sachs and JPMorgan Chase who sold those securities to their A-list clients probably convinced them with comments like, "Hey, if this market tanks—like the friggin' world comes to an end—we're not obligated to buy them back. Of course, that's never happened so don't worry about it. We've got your back."

Then the shit hit the fan. Most of the Wall Street firms who'd sold a lot of that overleveraged paper couldn't survive paying back angry customers their hundreds of millions of dollars. That's what took down Bear Stearns and ultimately led to the collapse of the credit markets. Private investors were pissed. "Hey, you sold me this shitty investment. What are you going to do about it?"

In my particular specialty, one of the hardest-hit markets was for insured tax-exempt auction rate securities. Bond insurance was crucial because it allowed investors—mostly high-net-worth individuals—to pass responsibility for the credit analyses on to the insurers. When the insurers faltered, billions in auction rate securities failed and many health systems were hit with maximum interest rates that topped 10 percent.

My clients began coming to us—this was happening everywhere on Wall Street—begging for short-term letters of credit and wanting to convert those auction-rate securities into something—anything—else. The banks, which rarely said no before, were now shutting the teller window to institutions that had been clients for decades. Those who did manage to get credit paid dearly and had to submit to tight financial covenants. So much for always putting clients first.

These market dynamics brought about major leadership changes within the banks, with the center of gravity shifting from banking toward the trading desks. That's when my boss took over the municipal bond department, including banking, credit, sales, trading, and underwriting—one individual leading an entire municipal bond department that was less than 5 percent of his overall responsibilities. It was part of CEO Jamie Dimon's goal to shed risk, avoid taking on any more, and to price scarce resources handsomely. That same thing was happening everywhere.

Clients who I had covered as a banker began calling trying to figure out what the hell was going on. One client in particular, originally a nonprofit billing and collections cooperative, had previously been extended credit facilities of up to $500 million, over-collateralized by their accounts receivable from their hospital clients. The hospitals, in return, got operating cash at an attractive, tax-exempt interest rate.

During the credit crisis, the billing services firm needed a letter of credit to support the debt in order to continue purchasing receivables—the firm's raw material. The CEO, who had once been a senior not-for-profit healthcare investment banker at other firms and a bit of a mentor to me, called one day, pleading, "Jesus, Mark. I'm begging you, man! We've got to have JPMorgan Chase renew our letter of credit. Otherwise, we're sunk."

But JPMorgan Chase no longer wanted any of it. Dimon had said he wanted "a fortress balance sheet." The firm also only wanted clients that would generate repeat business. They were the right decisions for JPMorgan Chase's shareholders but it made my job a nightmare, having to deliver the news to people I had been doing business with for many years that we were, in effect, putting them out of business. Without us, or some other source, they were insolvent. The collections firm did survive, but as a much smaller company with a different and successful business plan.

This was not unusual. Leading cancer centers, teaching hospitals, and other not-for-profit healthcare clients who had credit from JPMorgan Chase were now facing being shut down or financially crippled by the bank's refusal to renew their credit facilities, in large part because the traders who took over municipals didn't understand the credit quality of the clients. Inept, inexperienced, and ill-informed JPMorgan Chase managers new to public finance and their sycophantic analysts actually thought these legacy healthcare institutions were going to go out of business. It just didn't happen, but at the time it almost became a self-fulfilling prophecy when banks turned off the spigot.

This scary, unnecessary high-stakes game of musical chairs punished the innocent and, paradoxically, the most creditworthy customers. (Today, banks can't extend enough credit to these entities through direct purchases of bonds.) Even more maddening was that the new credit cops at the banks were celebrated as heroes for their risk management prowess and brilliance. Meanwhile, the new management team treated seasoned bankers who had painstakingly built that business like village idiots.

Thus began my demise. I would take these pleas and requests from clients starving for credit to my counterparts in sales, trading, and credit and they would look at me like I had two heads. They acted like aged beef and treated us like sausage.

Clients who were stiff-armed at JPMorgan Chase (or elsewhere) had to take what they could get—less and more expensive credit under more onerous terms that required them to restructure their debt. My clients had never really heard "No" before. When Wall Street was making money and markets were stable, it was always, "Yes," and what more can we do? Clients were treated royally. That was my job as a senior banker, to make each client feel like they were one of the firm's most important.

However, it was clear that the giant mutual fund and money managers—Vanguard, BlackRock, Fidelity, PIMCO—were more important. They could move a lot of bonds, stocks, currency hedges, credit and interest-rate swaps, trading twenty-four hours a day, seven days a week, around the globe. It was steady profitable business.

The heads of sales, trading, and underwriting considered clients who issued debt only once a year to be excess baggage to be pitched overboard to make the ship go faster. Meanwhile, the wealthy individuals who bought those failed auction-rate municipal bonds were fuming. They wanted to be made whole and they had the resources to hire phalanxes of lawyers to file blizzards of threatening lawsuits. It was a tense time.

The end for me finally came in March 2009 when my job was essentially eliminated. My boss, who was a trader, wanted one person—a trader—in charge of the entire municipal bond department, including public finance. He didn't say so, but my boss was probably sick of listening to the pitches of me and my senior team to save offices from being closed, to prevent bankers from being laid off and experienced law firms from being axed, or advocating for our issuer/borrower clients—the hospitals, the states, and the cities which needed our credit. His mandate was to minimize risk and focus on JPMorgan Chase's financial health and stock price. I don't remember him ever meeting a single public finance client.

On one of my last trips to the New York headquarters, he summoned me to his office. I knew this was to be the end and first called my wife, full of excitement, relief, and anxiety. She was supportive and gave her blessing. We had discussed this scenario many times.

Then, without pleasantries or misleading terminology, he informed me that he was consolidating municipals under sales, trading, and underwriting and that my current position was being eliminated. Then he asked me to take my former job as head of healthcare and higher education.

That was awkward. It was the position my hand-picked

successor had held for several years, doing an excellent job. It was time for me to go. I thanked him for a good run of twelve years at a venerable institution, the last year or so under his able leadership, and assured him I would make the transition as smooth as possible.

When your job is eliminated in the corporate world, you get to keep all your stock and you get a good severance package. After more than a year of hell, watching the dismantling of many key relationships and all that my colleagues and I had built, it was one of the happier moments of my career when I said, "Thanks, but I want out."

He was thoughtful and gracious even as he pushed back.

"Mark, I want you to go home, sleep on this, think about it for a week, talk to your wife but nobody else, and come back to me. You're very valuable. We want you to stay at JPMorgan. It kills me that I'm actually even having this conversation with you."

I conjured a family emergency so people would be less likely to bother me and flew home to Chicago. Diane and I took long walks, talking and thinking about the next steps.

CHAPTER 14:
"THIS IS A GREAT DAY"

One experience during my years as a Wall Street investment banker stands out as the most rewarding and also the most upsetting. In 1997 I worked for J.P. Morgan & Co. on facilitating the merger of two public institutions I hold in high regard. My alma mater, Penn State, had agreed to merge its Hershey Medical Center with Geisinger Health System.

It was such a perfect match that few people seriously questioned the logic or logistics. Each brought complementary institutional strengths to the marriage and they shared a strong commitment to their communities. Both Penn State and Geisinger had been founded and are still headquartered in small towns in the middle of Nowhere, Pennsylvania. The drive between them is seventy-five winding country miles through spectacular scenery. In summer the soaring walls of steep, heavily forested mountain ranges look like piles of green whipped cream. The valleys are dappled with working farms.

From the middle of Nowhere, Pennsylvania, to get to

Anywhere-At-All takes about three hours, whether it's Pittsburgh to the west or Philadelphia and New York to the east. Geisinger doesn't get a lot of drop-ins at its Danville offices. For anyone traveling from Anywhere-At-All to State College, Penn State's home town, it's a safe bet they have some compelling school-related business.

Penn State's sterling football history—the Nittany Lions, so named for a nearby mountain—is the legend most people have heard about. Between 1966 and 2011, the team fought its way into thirty-eight season-end college bowl playoffs out of a possible forty-four, all under coach Joe Paterno.

Not only was I a proud graduate of Penn State but my father sat on the committee in the Commonwealth's legislature that oversaw appropriations for the school's budget. Like most everyone else in Pennsylvania public life, he zealously supported the school. It was a treat to be able to talk with my dad about the deal and its implications.

Geisinger was for many years the most famous healthcare provider most Americans had never heard of. Like the much larger and older Mayo Clinic in Minnesota, or the Cleveland Clinic in Ohio, Geisinger began as, and still is, a physician-led provider. Mayo, Cleveland, and Geisinger are all large, preeminent, multi-specialty physician group practices.

Mayo was started by Dr. William Mayo and his two doctor sons in 1889. The Cleveland Clinic traces its origins to four Cleveland doctors, three of whom organized and ran a military hospital together in France during World War I.

Geisinger was started in 1915 by Abigail Geisinger, the wife of an iron magnate, George Geisinger. It was to be a regional medical center for an underserved area that included a lot of farmers, coal miners, and steel workers. The newly merged Penn State Geisinger Health System planned to move its headquarters seventy-five miles to Hershey, Pennsylvania, named for the chocolate baron, Milton Hershey, and his company. The merger brought under one roof 77 clinics and several hospitals, expanded coverage to 40 of Pennsylvania's 67 counties, and access to nearly 1,000 doctors.

It was the thrill of my career to work with my alma mater and with Geisinger, one of J.P. Morgan's most important public finance clients and one of the most enlightened, progressive hospital systems in the world. For example, Geisinger recently gambled on an experiment to offer patients a satisfaction-or-your-money-back guarantee on the deductibles they paid for their care. Industry wags said it was "a dumb idea" when it was introduced. After six months in effect, there had only been seventy-four refund requests and Geisinger had paid out just $80,000.

The merger unfolded in the middle of a financial crisis in the healthcare field. President Clinton had just signed into law the Balanced Budget Act of 1997, which reduced federal spending, including cuts of $110 billion in Medicare reimbursements for inpatient hospital services. Hospitals began losing money.

The day we brought the necessary bond issues for the Penn State–Geisinger merger to market, Allegheny Health, Education and Research Foundation, another Pennsylvania hospital system, filed for bankruptcy protection. I was on J.P. Morgan's trading floor in New York when the news came across the wires. It was traumatic, a black swan—for a tax-exempt health system to actually go broke seemed impossible until it happened.

Municipal bonds are considered nearly as safe as US government bonds. Healthcare bonds are regarded as high-yielding munis, but absolutely safe and secure investments as well. Now it looked like all our hard work was at risk.

Allegheny was an aberration, the result of a perfect storm of Wall Street bankers who had overloaded it with debt and overreaching management which had gone on an acquisition spending spree. Investment bankers get paid per transaction only if they close the deal, so if anyone had doubts at the time they kept them to themselves.

In order to save the Penn State–Geisinger inaugural debt issuance, we scrambled to explain to potential investors that just because Allegheny was in Pennsylvania didn't mean there was also a problem at Geisinger or Penn State. In the end, J.P. Morgan took the courageous step of buying the bonds with very few investors participating—a true underwriting—and selling them off over a period of weeks.

The merger became official at a signing ceremony at Geisinger in July 1997. Penn State President Graham Spanier signed the papers that formalized the relationship. Dr. C. McCollister Evarts, formerly president and chief executive officer of Hershey Medical Center, declared, "This is a great day."

Everything seemed to go smoothly for about two years. The full merger would take much longer, especially in a period of financial turmoil. There were the usual issues of redundancy, power shifts, and layoffs that were blamed on the merger instead of on economic conditions.

Gradually the combination began to show me a political side of Penn State I hadn't encountered before. There were early rumblings that the dean of the medical school, who was in charge of the pre-merged academic medical center and who made all of the appointments to the department chairs, was upset because he was losing his clout.

Two years after the merger, Penn State president Spanier was rumored to be concerned about how the merger was threatening the academic and research mission of the university's College of Medicine. The medical school had suffered a flurry of defections by dozens of doctors and researchers, leaving some departments short-staffed. About a thousand employees at Hershey Medical Center signed petitions opposing the merger. None of this struck me as particularly alarming. These were typical growing pains when two different cultures are put together.

A decade earlier Penn State had joined the Big Ten Athletic Conference, which meant I was able to go to more games now that the Lions were playing Northwestern, Illinois, Wisconsin, Michigan and Michigan State. One Saturday in October 1999, Penn State was playing Illinois in Champaign–Urbana. Diane and I were invited to a Friday night fundraising reception in Chicago with Spanier. (That's the same Spanier who presided during the years that Jerry Sandusky was molesting boys in the Penn State locker room, and who was fired in 2011 and indicted for perjury and failure to report suspected child abuse.)

Diane and I were going to the theater that evening so we were leaving immediately after the cocktail hour. Before we left, feeling content and quite at home, I went up to Spanier and reached out to shake his hand.

"Dr. Spanier, I'm Mark Melio. My father's in the state legislature and I'm a Penn State alum. I'm proud to say that

I manage the healthcare and higher-education investment banking group at JPMorgan Chase and we executed the financings around the merger." I paused, waiting for a warm smile and a congratulatory remark.

Instead, Spanier's forehead crumpled and panic showed in his eyes. He took my arm and pulled me closer, whispering, "Listen, I have to talk to you. This thing has to be undone. We have to get out of that terrible deal."

A spasm gripped my midsection, like I had been punched. I had no clue what to say. I could see he wasn't joking.

He continued, "Listen, I want you to call my assistant and get on my calendar as soon as possible. You need to come meet me on campus, because we've got to figure out how to get out of this deal."

My mood was ruined and all through the theater performance all I could think was, What the hell was that?! The complex deal had been consummated. All the details had been worked out. It was two years into the merger. Now all of a sudden Graham Spanier wanted a quickie divorce.

The next day I called my contacts at Geisinger. "Yeah, it's bad," they said. "These people really want to de-merge with us." That's a word you rarely hear. Unscrambling an egg would be easier.

The following week I arranged to fly out to State College to meet with Spanier, but when winter weather closed LaGuardia Airport I hired a Town Car. I took a colleague with me and for four hours we sat in the back seat putting together a presentation on why a de-merger would be unwise and imprudent for Penn State's medical school and Hershey Medical Center.

We met Spanier in a private dining room at the Nittany

Lion Inn, the formal hotel on campus, and realized very quickly that he had completely caved in to his medical school dean—a doctor who was angry that he was losing his power. On November 18, 1999, the board voted to undo the merger. In large part because of the dean's personal agenda, Penn State–Geisinger lost the opportunity to become an even more amazing health system and an even greater asset to Pennsylvania sooner.

Later, when it came out that Spanier had failed to challenge Paterno when Sandusky's child abuse crimes became known, it made sense to me. He didn't stand up to others in power. He wanted out of the deal and didn't give a damn whether it cost the university, essentially Pennsylvania taxpayers, $50 million or $250 million. On the investment banking side, we had to figure out what happens after you sell a bond based on a projected payment stream that doesn't quite pan out.

To be completely fair, the Penn State–Geisinger debacle happened during a spell of mega-mergers, de-mergers, successes, and collapses among giant hospital systems. During that same period, my friend Lawrence Furnstahl of the University of Chicago Medical Center spent two years as CFO of the newly created UCSF Stanford Health System, a result of the merger of the University of California San Francisco Medical Center and Stanford Health System. That deal also blew up and after two years the merger was undone.

It turns out that combining two academic medical centers is a colossal feat. Furnstahl later explained that the Stanford doctors and the UCSF doctors were supposed to be sharing profits. But only Stanford was profitable so money had to be transferred from Stanford to UCSF.

Furnstahl said, "The Stanford doctors would just as soon have taken all of the money they earned and thrown it into San Francisco Bay instead of sharing it with the UCSF docs."

The good news is that Geisinger has continued to grow, its reputation is as strong as it ever was, its financial condition is sound, and now I sit on its side of the table when advice is required. There have been many customers I've worked with over the past three decades that have rewarded and confirmed my career choice. Geisinger ranks at or near the top of that list. It's in Pennsylvania, where I grew up and got my education. Its directors and executives are down to earth—I have left more than one meeting with a container of fresh farm products. Its market is quintessentially American, rural and without pretense. And, like Mayo and the Cleveland Clinic, it stayed true to its mission.

CHAPTER 15:
THE SCORPION
AND THE FROG

You can't walk away from a high-paying, master-of-the-universe job at one of the largest investment banks in the world without going through some withdrawal symptoms.

As soon as word got out that I was leaving JPMorgan Chase, I got cordial invitations to talk with the heads of public finance at many other major banks. All were more interested in picking my brain about JPMorgan Chase and former Bear Stearns bankers than in recruiting an expensive, older guy whose resume made them or their senior staff feel threatened.

I'm a true "client guy," a banker who dotes on his clients. Being a client guy meant that wherever I landed many of my customers would likely follow. They trusted me more than the bank, a fact that every so often made me feel pride tinged with a little guilt.

The prima donna in me did miss the perks. When you have to travel frequently for work it's not so bad when you're nearly always in first class, staying at the best hotels, always being met by a car and driver assigned to you until you're safely delivered back to the airport for your next flight. In between I wined and dined clients at the best restaurants and took them to the best sporting and performance events where we had the best seats. I liked the majority of those people and embraced their goals of obtaining the lowest cost of capital, which in turn would provide better, more accessible and affordable healthcare.

And yet it was so messed up. At least that's how I felt afterward. I had been well compensated over more than two decades for enabling Goldman Sachs and JPMorgan Chase to siphon off countless hundreds of millions from clients as they passed through the system. That's a bit exaggerated, but it describes my cynical state of mind at the time. On one hand, I was proud of all I had accomplished but felt betrayed by the institutions that had taken advantage of relationships I had cultivated largely on trust. On the other, I had been a willing accomplice and enabler.

In my heart I had known all of this as it was happening but I had been too busy putting out fires to contemplate the big picture. During my last two years at JPMorgan Chase, I was responsible for steering the firm's public finance business through the second-worst financial crisis in modern history. The acquisition, dismantling, and integration of Bear Stearns required me to do things that are not in my nature— eliminating the jobs of more than 150 of my peers, closing offices, firing law firms, and shutting the window on all charitable contributions. Hardest of all, I had to tell my loyal long-term clients why their "trusted advisor" bank had pulled the rug out from under them when they needed us most.

I was soon to turn fifty years old, so I was looking for a position that would likely be my last job before retirement. It was important that I do something uplifting, if not noble.

Continuing to bring home those outsized paychecks was alluring. That would mean grinding the same old sausage, just in a different factory—assuming I could find someone who'd hire a banker with my background. As an independent financial advisor, I might see my income dip but I'd be free to act solely with my clients' best interests in mind, to advocate as a fiduciary without reservation or inhibition.

Just as I was wrapping up my work at JPMorgan Chase, the Obama administration sent a series of proposed bills to Congress that were part of a comprehensive effort to reform Wall Street. It was the early stages of what became the Dodd–Frank Wall Street Reform and Consumer Protection Act, named for its cosponsors, Senator Chris Dodd of Connecticut and Representative Barney Frank of Massachusetts. When all was said and done, Dodd–Frank was the most extensive overhaul of the financial system since the early 1930s.

One goal was to clear up conflict-of-interest confusion in public finance—issuers assuming their banks were giving them unbiased advice and thinking the banks were watching their backs. Instead, those trusted banks had steered many municipalities into overly complex financial structures and high-risk derivatives that made a lot of other people rich but caused huge loss positions for issuers and investors alike.

Among the proposals was a requirement that CFOs and

other fiduciary officials of municipal bond issuers (public institutions) be required to sign a letter acknowledging that whatever investment bank they are doing business with is not independent. That proposal became law and now clients have to formally acknowledge that underwriters have no fiduciary duty to them and that the underwriters' interests differ from their own. That's how effectively Wall Street had obscured the truth. For many clients who were otherwise competent financial professionals, having to acknowledge these facts in black and white was quite a revelation.

A related proposal being bandied about was to establish a special category of independent, registered municipal advisors for public finance, much like independent advisors that individual investors turn to for advice. There wouldn't be million-dollar bonuses at the end of the year, but I thought I might be able to build a business out of telling the truth and saving public institutions from costly decisions.

My client and friend of several decades, Lawrence Furnstahl at University of Chicago Medical Center (UCMC), had issued billions of dollars of debt in his career and was eager to have me—an expert who understands the banks culturally and organizationally—on his side. Furnstahl is an ardent foodie and likens the experience of having a pro on his team to one he had in Chicago when he went out to eat one night at a hot new restaurant. He invited a friend who is an experienced and successful owner of high-end restaurants. The reservation was under Funstahl's name so the hostess was stunned when he showed up with Mary Beth Liccioni, a marquee restaurateur in the Windy City.

"It was like we'd casually waltzed in off the street with the

Queen of England. The staff were falling all over themselves trying to make everything perfect. And we got an insider's take from her about the food and how it was prepared. It's a little like that when we visit banks now because everyone knows Mark and they step up their game. They know they can't get away with the same old same old."

As much as I knew, being on the outside looking in had its revelations for me too. As an independent financial advisor, my job is to make sure bond issues are not excessively oversubscribed, that the banks are selling the bonds to reputable retail and institutional investors, and that my client is getting the lowest interest rate they can under the prevailing conditions. The interest rate calculation is where things get slippery because underwriters aggressively manage expectations.

On the first bond issue I did as a financial advisor for the UCMC, the board of trustees—inarguably a financially sophisticated client—sent Furnstahl and me to New York for the pricing of a $75 million fixed-rate deal. It was funding for the first stage of a new $500 million hospital pavilion. The board's instructions were, "Don't be a single dollar oversubscribed. Get it exactly right."

At the end of the pre-order period, the interest rate appeared to be very attractive for the hospital (low) but there were orders for roughly $87 million—we were $12 million oversubscribed. Because the financing was part of a larger program, we raised the dollar amount of the bond issue to $87 million to match the orders. We high-fived each other. We were geniuses! We weren't a dollar oversubscribed. We could go back to the board with a success story at a low rate—at the time around 5.5 percent.

Furnstahl called me one morning, puzzling over why some doctors at the hospital were eagerly seeking his advice about whether to buy UCMC's bonds, which they said were priced to yield 4.75 percent, three quarters of a percent (75 basis points) below the initial offering yield. When I checked the secondary market trades, I found that hundreds of transactions had been executed beginning within minutes and continuing for a couple of days after the original sale at a lower rate. Our 5.5 percent bonds had been flipped for a profit, just like a stock IPO, at 4.75 percent. That spread of 0.75% belonged to University of Chicago Medical Center but it went into the pockets of JPMorgan Chase's favored investors.

On top of that, the secondary purchasers of the 4.75 percent bonds were turning around and offering them to individual investors at between 4.25 percent and 4.50 percent. In the end, this flipping business had effectively screwed the hospital out of a few million dollars.

Besides the haircut, the flipping exposed the hospital to the risk of stirring up the IRS, which gets cranky if tax-exempt bond yields look inflated. The higher the interest rate, the more lost tax revenue. Flipping also infuriates the SEC on behalf of the Aunt Berthas whose bonds are manipulatively priced against them.

When confronted with this evidence, the underwriting and syndicate desk claimed they had no control over flipping, but we didn't believe it. We had been assured of a successful and coordinated marketing effort to a vast "institutional and retail investor base." It had all sounded so good. Furnstahl and I summoned JPMorgan Chase's lead underwriter and bankers to the executive offices at the Medical Center and demanded to know, "What the hell happened?"

The underwriter squirmed a little and with hands outstretched in supplication said, "Hey, we have to sell bonds and 5.5 percent was what it took. And look how much extra capital you raised. This happens. It's always been this way."

It was a lame answer and reminded me of the fable about a scorpion and a frog meeting on a stream bank. The scorpion asks the frog to carry it across to the other side.

"Of course not. You'll sting me," the frog says.

The scorpion promises, "I won't. I just want to get to the other side. Why would I sting you? If I did, we'd both die."

The frog agrees to let the scorpion ride on his back and, sure enough, in the middle of the stream it stings the frog.

As the frog begins to die and sink beneath the water, it cries out, "Why did you do that? Now you will drown, too."

"I'm a scorpion. It's in my nature."

EPILOGUE

It doesn't have to be that way—scorpions always stinging frogs because that's just how it is. When the University of Chicago Medical Center was ready to go back into the market for additional funding a few months later, we ran a competitive bid process limited to three broker-dealers Furnstahl had worked with on prior deals.

Healthcare bond issues are rarely competitively bid, mainly because investment banks discourage competition to protect their fees. We told Wells Fargo, Barclays, and JPMorgan Chase, "Give us quotes for the bonds. Whoever comes in with the lowest rate gets the deal."

In other words, we told them they had to take on some of the risk by buying the bonds and guaranteeing the rate in advance. The firms spluttered and blustered. "Melio, you're dreaming. This won't work. We can't do that. It's the worst idea we've ever heard. It's never been done. It hasn't been thought through. Is this some kind of stunt?"

But it did work. When we reviewed the secondary market trades on the subsequent competitive deal, instead of hundreds there weren't even a handful. The secondary market spread was negligible to nonexistent and the primary market spread was the narrowest it had been in months. It was perfect.

Seven or so years later, I look back on what I learned about Wall Street's culture during my career, what's happened since the credit crisis, and what's going on today. The technology has evolved, the deal toys are smaller, and there are more forms to sign, but Wall Street is still a python pit.

I've seen underwriters allocate bonds to themselves ahead of legitimate retail and institutional orders. I've seen premeditated flips to favored buy-side accounts minutes after the bonds were free to trade, then repurchased by the trading desks and flipped again, aiding and abetting the entire scheme. I've also seen brokers posture trading accounts and hedge funds as fictitious Mom and Pop retail accounts with $1 million orders and made-up zip codes just to get first priority on the bonds. And it hasn't stopped.

Government can regulate all it wants, but before the ink dries on a new rule, somewhere in some back office a bunch of bankers, lawyers, and math geniuses are engineering a way around it.

I'd spent much of 2008 on the trading floor dealing with auction failures, downgrades of municipal bond insurers, short-term variable rate bonds being put back to the banks, and then bank failures. In the process I got a close look at the current cadre of financial advisors and realized none of them had a clue how to navigate these uncharted waters. Most had been financial advisors their entire careers. Few had banking experience or even the most basic securities license—the Series 7—which assesses the competency of an entry-level associate or analyst to perform his or her job as a general securities representative.

Upon leaving Wall Street, my hunch was that sophisticated clients would be interested in hiring a financial advisor with a passionate team that has twenty-plus years of hands-on investment banking experience to help shepherd them through their financings. As the saying goes, Bigger isn't better. Bigger is bigger. Better is better.

I discussed the idea of switching roles (from banker to advisor) with some prospective clients and got exciting feedback. Together we would collaborate on disruptive innovation—a mutually supportive conspiracy to refocus and center attention from the banks back to the clients. Everything would be creative, transparent, and competitive to produce the best outcomes and lowest costs of capital. At the very least, we would no longer be held hostage by investment bankers peddling advice that earned them the biggest profits, nor sales and trading desks that sold bonds to select investors who would immediately flip them for a quick buck.

New technologies and disruptive innovations are gradually making the traditional Wall Street setup obsolete, which will benefit issuers, borrowers, and thus all of us. It's exciting to be part of it.

ACKNOWLEDGEMENTS

During my journey through public finance on Wall Street (at least the part through Goldman Sachs and JPMorgan Chase) to where I am now, I have had the pleasure to work alongside sincere, dedicated not-for-profit executives, public servants, bankers, and lawyers who are intelligent, animated, adept, altruistic, committed and consummate professionals. In some ways this is our collective story.

I have also worked alongside some bastards. This is their story, too.

Although this story highlights many of the shortcomings of public finance, I believe that when done right—that is, when the issuers' and borrowers' interests truly come first—it is an honorable profession.

Not only was I an investment banker for nearly twenty-five years, but for most of that time I also headed the healthcare and higher education group and, for some of it, all of public finance. In addition to being a top revenue producer myself, I managed teams of bankers, encouraging them to bring in more and more revenue, firing those that were not generating enough revenue, hiring others who I thought had more revenue potential, and promoting and paying significant bonuses to those bankers who produced the most revenue. I didn't just have a ringside seat, I was in the ring itself.

Before I get to the story, I want to thank my wife, Diane, for her boundless support, honesty, and encouragement, for keeping me focused on what really mattered, and for being my best friend. I also thank our children, Paul, Anna, Julia, and Pelle, for their enthusiasm, insight, and inspiration. I thank my grandparents, parents, brother, and sister for making me feel there was nothing I couldn't do.

I thank my Melio & Company partners and colleagues, former and current, for their confidence in joining a small start-up and then making it successful beyond everyone's expectations.

I thank many of my former colleagues at Goldman Sachs and J.P. Morgan & Co. (now JPMorgan Chase) for the camaraderie we shared along the way. There are many more memories and stories that didn't make it into the book than did.

Many of the clients I came to know so well while I was working at Goldman Sachs & Co. and JPMorgan Chase have honored me by continuing to rely on my advice at Melio & Company. The collective support and loyalty of our clients made Melio & Company's existence possible and thus this book, which I hope will shed light on how we finance our public needs and how we might continue doing it better in the future.

I would like to thank Louisiana Ramos and Drew DeBakker for the excellent artwork and my son Paul for his wisdom and astute insights.

Lastly, my thanks to Foster Winans, without whom this story might never have been told.

CPSIA information can be obtained
at www.ICGtesting.com
Printed in the USA
BVHW03s1939260718
522744BV00001B/49/P